The Teachings of Human Beings and of God Inspired by the Holy Spirit

The Teachings of Human Beings and of God Inspired by the Holy Spirit

Inspirational Writings of Human Beings and of God

Kristen Marie Player

Strategic Book Publishing and Rights Co.

Strategic Book Publishing & Rights Co., LLC
USA | Singapore
www.sbpra.net

For information about special discounts for bulk purchases, please contact Strategic Book Publishing and Rights Co. Special Sales, at bookorder@sbpra.net.

ISBN: 978-1-68235-472-8

Acknowledgement

Paul my Husband Wilma Paul's Mum Sandra Janet David Aaron Jane & Raphael Belinda Mutiso.

Once you believe that you can do anything that your heart desires you will be successful. Don't let anything bring you down. Your life is here to be enjoyed. Be happy and don't worry about anything. Life is what you make it. Treasure every moment of your life. Appreciate people who you are close to. Go on to achieve what you have always wanted to achieve. Believe in yourself and have high love and respect for yourself. Hang in there you will feel better. You are not a failure if you don't make it. You are a success because you tried. Hang in there and keep on trying. Don't give up until you are satisfied. Keep on trying you will succeed with everything.

Keep on striving to achieve your goals. By never ever giving up hope. There will be rough times but on the other hand there will be good times as well. Think of yourself as a winner and that's what you will be. Never let anyone bring you down. Have high respect and love for yourself. Forgive those people who hurt you unfairly. Be kind to those people who you think are trying to upset you. Learn to stand up for yourself in assertive ways when you need to. Value every day and appreciate what you have got. Make the most of everything each day. You will get what you will give. Do kind deeds always.

Accept yourself as you are. Be happy and don't worry about anything. Be grateful for everything you have. Show your love to those people who you are close to. By supporting them by openly listening to them. Do what you love to do. Spend time with people who make you happy. Have an optimistic view on as many things as you can. That way you will feel a lot better about yourself. Love and enjoy every day of your life. Create a meaningful rewarding life.

Follow your dreams and doors will open for you. Always show your respect to those people who you are close to. By giving them the support you think they need. Have an open ear to other opportunities in your life. Go down avenues that will suit you. That you think will be right for you to excel in your life. Do what is best for you in every situation. Always learn from all of your mistakes.

Have a full life that way you won't have any regrets later on. Do what you love to do. Try new things that you think you might like and enjoy. Make the most of every single day of your life. That way you will feel satisfied. Rise above feelings of despair. Have enough strength to carry on in your life. Don't wait for things to happen to you. Get out there and make your ambitions aspirations dreams happen. Respect people by showing your kindness towards them. Try not to let anyone affect the way you are feeling. Always have confidence courage healthy self esteem within yourself.

Always have faith within yourself. Every day count your blessings. Accept the way how things turn out. You get back what you give out. You can't change people but you can change yourself. Use your time wisely and productively. Make the most of every day. Have the motivation to do well in your life. By succeeding with your desires. Face your fears and all will go well for you. Be brave and courageous and things will come your way. Pull yourself out of feelings of despair and frustration. Everything passes in good time. Time heals it all.

Work on fulfilling your days so you are positive and content with your achievements. Always have hope when you feel like you are stuck with your worries. Then you will have a positive outcome in the end. We all have to go through the bad to get to the good. Keep on trying hard every day and strive to do your best. Take what you think are worthwhile opportunities and go for it. Don't let good opportunities pass you by. Have an open mind for self improvement. By having a better style of quality of your life. Always remind yourself that there are good things around the corner. Good things will come.

That will come your way in the right time. Be patient with yourself and other people. That way you will be able to make wiser decisions on a better level. Be determined to do the best you possibly can in your life. Do what you enjoy and love doing the most. Don't look at your life as a big chore. Be positive and enthusiastic in your attitude. You will feel a lot better in good time. Create a joyful and happy life.

No one has the power to create unhappiness for you. Only if you let them. Don't let anyone affect the way you are feeling. By making you feel hurt and upset. You have the strength to make a very good and rewarding life for yourself. Accept the good with the bad. Always forgive and love those people who hurt and upset you. Each of us have the power to create a good life for ourselves. Never give up on anyone and anything. Always have hope for a good and prosperous future that lies ahead. Try to be optimistic and always hope for the best. Always speak positive kind nice lovely good loving words.

You have the strength to carry on in your life. Don't let anyone bring you down. Be happy with who you are. Try your very best with what you want to achieve. Have hope for good things to come your way. Never give up on anything. Life is wonderful. Life is a superb gift. We are all taken care of our Father God Almighty who is in The Kingdom of Heaven. Answering all of our prayers. Be happy and don't worry about anything. The world is your oyster. Do your very best with everything in your life. Try try try again and you will succeed.

Organize to have good times with your friends. No one has any kind of power over you at all. Always do positive kind loving good fair just deeds for everyone every day of your life. Life might seem like a long hard road to travel on. Really we are all only here on this Earth for a short period of time. Make the most of every single day of your life. The challenges you are faced with are stepping stones for you to become a much better resilient courageous stronger experienced individual. Be a great listener and a wonderful communicator.

Treasure every day of your life. Always be appreciative grateful thankful for everything God has given you in your life. Believe in yourself and know that you are just as good as everyone else. Never dwell on feelings of despair. You don't have to seek anyone's approval of yourself. It is important to be comfortable enough within yourself. To make all of your own choices and decisions in your life.

No one has got any kind of control over you. You are your own boss in your life. Remember to forgive and love those people who try to hurt you badly. Always build a wonderful meaningful fruitful blessed rewarding life for yourself. Every day have great gratitude with everything you do. Look forward to what you have got planned ahead of you. Always be around people who lift you up by bringing out the best in you. Don't be around people who bring you down. Don't let anything bring you down in your life. Always have hope and faith in yourself. Do everything your heart desires for in your life.

Hang in there until things get better. Think positively about yourself and other people. Know that you can handle anything that comes your way because you can. Never give up on anything. Be motivated and determined to do your very best in everything you do. You have the potential to achieve anything that you want to so make the most of things every day. Know that you have got what it takes to make a great life for yourself because you can if you try. Do what it takes to have a fulfilling wonderful meaningful knowledgeable prosperous life

You can create a wonderful life for yourself. Never forget this. Always try your very best for yourself in every situation you put yourself in. Don't let anyone undermined your confidence. You have the power not to let this happen. Remind yourself of all of the good thing and good points you have in your life and that will see you through. Don't depend on anyone for anything because you have the strength and determination to cope with anything and everything that comes your way. Always hope for the very best in your life. Be positive joyful.

Always hope for the very best in your life. Know that you have got what it takes to make it and you can survive the challenges you have to deal with. Organize for yourself a wonderful future. Full of what you always wanted to do and be. Remember to forgive those people that hurt you. Follow your heart in everything you do. Be kind to people and show your respect and consideration and compassion to those people who you know and trust and who you are close to.

You can cope with anything and everything that comes your way. Always remember this. Be happy with who you are and don't let anyone discourage you with anything in your life. Go on to achieve what you have always wanted to achieve. Remember to always take pride in yourself by showing respect to those people who appreciate you. Always hang in there with whatever you are faced with in your life. Have enough strength to survive life's challenges. Never give up on anything. Keep on working hard to be determined and motivated in everything you do. You will enjoy your life with a positive attitude.

Also work on being patient with yourself and other people. Persevere with everything you do in your life. Keep on being persistent with the challenges in your life. Then things will turn out for you for the better. Remember to always hope for a better time to come when you feel a bit down. Everything passes in good time. The world is your oyster. Do what you think you are capable of doing. Don't set unrealistic goals for yourself. Life is wonderful.

Do what you think you can manage. What you think you will be able to do. Keep busy with the things that inspire you that you enjoy doing. Make your life good. Always learn from your mistakes. Be around people who encourage you who understand you. Go on to achieve what you have always wanted to achieve. Don't waste any of your days. Have full days with work rest and play. Enjoy your life because you only get one shot at it. Make the most of every day.

To achieve anything in your life you will be faced with challenges. It is good for your personal growth to look at challenges in a positive way. You can get through any difficult circumstance and learn a great deal from it. It takes courage to admit your faults to change what you don't like about the things you might be doing. All of us make mistakes it is those of us who will go a long way who learn from the mistakes we make. There are always new things to learn every day from the mistakes you make. Every day is a gift and blessing.

Try to be optimistic as you possibly can in as many areas of your life. When you feel a bit down tell yourself what positive things you have achieved in the past 6 months. Congratulate yourself for your consistency strength determination. Give appreciation to those who support and encourage you in your life. Never take anything for granted. Set realistic goals for yourself each day that you think you will be able to achieve. Then once you have achieved your goals reward yourself. By doing something that you think you will enjoy doing. Always believe in yourself with everything you will ever do.

Organize for yourself a place where only you alone will go each day. A place that is only yours and take the time at this place. To reflect over what you have done and achieved for the day. Be adventurous with planning your days. Don't wait around for things to happen to you. Be courageous and make things happen for yourself. Do what you love to do. You are your own boss in your life. You have choices with where you like to be. You always make your own decisions.

What you would like to be. What you would like to do. So make the most of everyday and start getting organised. Be motivated and determined to do well. Do your very best and don't let anyone bring you down. Don't let anyone question the person you are. Be proud of who you are. Be grateful for how you are and what you have got. Always hang onto every bit of strength you have within yourself.

To get through any difficult time in your life. Hold onto the good memories you have. That you yourself have achieved. Never let anyone bring you down to a level of frustration. Try to rise above these feelings of despair. No one can do this to you only if you give them the power to do this. Believe in yourself know that you have the potential to achieve anything that you could possibly ever want to achieve. Try not to let people affect your self esteem. Know that you have got what it takes to have a good life. Create interesting things to do for yourself. Try to be as optimistic as you can even when things seem tough. You will get there with all of your dreams.

Be patient with yourself and you will reap the benefits. Show consistency and perseverance in your work. Accept that you will have challenges to get through in your every day life. Don't be too hard on yourself if things don't turn out the way you would of liked them to. Respect those people who appreciate you. Always be determined to do your very best in everything you do. Organise for yourself things that you enjoy doing every day. Give yourself credit when you have gotten through any difficult time. At work or wherever it maybe during your days. You will make it through.

Always have persistence and strength to get through things. With what you yourself would like to achieve. Hang in there with everything. Keep on trying to achieve your goals. No one can affect the way you are feeling that's only if you let them. Stick with people who give you praise and who uplift your spirits. Don't mix with people who bring you down and who like to dump their negative stuff onto you a lot. People like this are insecure within themselves. When you find people who encourage you by lifting you up in positive ways. You will always feel good uplifted elated in yourself.

Then you will be a much more joyful peaceful happier person. You will become like the people who you associate with the most in your life. Have a rich life full of what you like and enjoy doing the most. Don't waste any of your days. Live your days to the fullest always. Be around people who make you feel good about yourself. Life is too short to be worrying about things. Get on with it and fulfill your goals. Then you will reap the rewarding benefits. You will be happy.

Be proud of who you are and people will want to be with you in your company. Do productive things every day. Don't waste your days doing unproductive things. Make the most of every single day. Follow your heart always make appropriate decisions. Never go out of your way to be cruel and nasty to anyone. Stick with those people who don't judge you and who never bring you down. Treat people well. Always have love and respect for yourself and other people.

Do the very best you possibly can in your life. You can create a really wonderful life for yourself always remember this. Plan your days doing things that you want and enjoy doing. Be grateful for what you have in your life. Show respect to your family and friends. Appreciate them for the care and kindness they provide you with. Have an open mind to further your possibilities of success in your life. Love every single day of your life. Be thankful grateful appreciative for everything you have. Always do what's right for you and everyone.

Fulfill your dreams by achieving your goals. Be consistent with your desires of your heart. Do what you have always wanted to do and be. Have gratitude towards your family and friends. Appreciate them for their achievements and love. You are the captain of your own ship in your life. Make your life just how you want it to be. By doing what you are good at and gifted in. Be determined to achieve your goals. Start off small and work your way up to a point of success. Be happy with who you are. Get involved with what you are interested in.

You will find you will grow in confidence that way. Be around positive people who want the very best for you. Keep active during your days. Every day is a gift so why not make the most of it while it is there. Be grateful for everything in your life. You will always reap the rewards and benefits. Take the time for yourself to do what you want to do. Always be positive and content with you are. You will find that people will be attracted to you. When you are happy within yourself.

Create a really wonderful life for yourself full of what you like to do. Make sure you choose your friends very carefully and wisely. Fill your life up with things you enjoy doing. Do something you have always wanted to do that you haven't done before. Be honest with yourself with what you want to achieve. Set realistic goals for yourself. That way you will find you will be able to achieve them. Be respectful considerate kind loving good fair just. To those people who you really appreciate and adore. Don't put any kind of unwanted pressure.

On yourself if you haven't succeeded with achieving your goals. Give yourself good time and eventually you will succeed with achieving your goals very well. When one door closes then another door will open. Have courage and determination to achieve. All that you have ever dreamed to have happen in your life. Live every day to the fullest. Surround yourself with positive and encouraging people. Who want to live their lives. To the fullest and who want the very best for you. Work towards having a positive and happy existence always.

The past is irrelevant. The only important this about the past. Is that you have learn't from your mistakes. Don't spend any time dwelling on negative things. Fill your mind up with positive and loving thoughts. You will feel better about yourself that way. Focus on the present moment. With what you want to achieve. Establish good friendships with people who you connect well with. Offer support to those people who you care for. You have a lot to look forward to in the future. Your future will be full of lots of wonderful surprises that you will benefit from enormously. Everything you want will happen.

Have an open mind to better your opportunities. Be active and get involved with what you love to do and enjoy doing every day. Be persistent with your desires. Have a healthy lifestyle. Spend time working out what you have always wanted to do and be. Encourage your close friends with their goals. Keep on working hard to get where you want to be. Be grateful appreciative thankful for every day of your life you live. Work towards fulfilling your goals. Have consistency with your work and activities. Be thankful and grateful for the people in your life. Your true friends will always love you.

Who support you and who are always there for you through the thick and the thin. Have good days doing what you like to do. Enjoy the moments you have on your own. Anything that you want to achieve is attainable. If you really want to do something then you will go ahead and do it. Once you set you mind toward achieving your goals.

Then there is nothing stopping you. Don't let anything ever come in the way. Of you achieving what you what you have always wanted to achieve. Have time to look after yourself. Be proud of who you are. Be grateful what you have your health and be grateful that you are alive. No one can have a negative affect on you that's only if you let them. When you are in a situation where you find yourself clashing with another person. Never raise your voice at them. It takes two people to have an argument. Instead learn to concentrate on what you are doing. Be really good at what you do as a job and activities.

Learn to deal with the person if they confront you. With kindness goodness compassion politeness. Never ever get angry. Never involve any other authority figure only in emergencies. That way your boss won't see you as a nuisance. Be good at your job. Don't pay too much attention to your colleagues. Instead concentrate on what you are getting paid to do in your job. Be the master of your own life always. Take hold of everything you will ever do. Help yourself. In every situation you are in learn how to handle yourself.

In the most productive ways. Hold your head up high. With confidence and gratitude. Don't let anything get on top of you ever. You have the control to not let yourself get upset or hurt. Enjoy every day of your life. People will be drawn to you when you show them respect consideration compassion kindness goodness love fairness. People like to be thought of. When you show interest thoughtfulness enthusiasm towards people. People will really appreciate you acting this way towards them. You will receive blessings and rewards in return. Do good good will happen.

Love your family and friends. As much as you love yourself and all will go well for you. Be grateful thankful appreciative that you are alive. Continue enjoying and loving your life. Our bodies minds spirits are full of God's challenging love. We are apart of God in Spirit. Our reason for hardship in difficult times. Is so we learn to grow as people. We learn to turn to God in the difficult times. God is there.

God is always with us. God knows everything about us. God will always and forever keep you safe and well protected. Once you learn how to Honour your Father God Almighty. You will find how The Lord Your God is working in your life. When we are faced with people. Who are short tempered towards us. It helps us to be stronger and more forgiving. Never ever let anyone undermined your confidence. You are worth so much more than you could possibly ever know. Be kind to yourself. Do things that make you feel good.

Practice loving and forgiving those people who hurt you always. Continue praying for your family and friends and love your enemies. God is with you. Never let anyone make you feel down. Rise above such negative people like this. Say nice kind loving good words towards them. Don't hold any grudges towards anyone life is too short for this. Be kind to people and do nice gestures for your family and friends. You have a lot to look forward to in your life.

Keep on enjoying every day. When you are smiling then other people will smile with you. You have nothing to fear because God is here with us in Spirit. God will always be with us in Spirit here on Earth. God is very forgiving and understanding. God absolutely loves and adores each and everyone of us. God will protect us from evil. God will turn bad into good. God will always be there for you.

God will help us to be loving and forgiving towards each other. God wants the very best for all of us. Most of all God wants us to be joyful peaceful happy content. Don't spend your time worrying about anything. Life is too short for this. Be thoughtful of other people. Do a nice gesture for someone. This person will really appreciate this. Always be kind and good to yourself. Practice telling yourself positive and loving thoughts every day. Remember to always love and forgive people who hurt you. Never ever give up on anything. Have the motivation to succeed by having a full life. Life is what you make it. Plan to do things to look forward to with your family and friends. Always be there for your family and friends. Do kind deeds always.

Never put yourself down. Tell yourself you are a good and worthwhile person. Who has a lot of potential and ability. Create a wonderful life for yourself. Fulfill your dreams. Make the most of every single day of your life. Be courageous and brave within yourself in safe ways. Treat people well just the way you would like to be treated. What goes around comes around. What you give out you will get back. If you give out kindness goodness love compassion to people. Then that's what you will receive in return from people.

If you think someone has treated you badly. Smile at them and say have a good day to them. Never be angry towards anyone. Don't have a bitter heart. If you do that that will just make you feel miserable. Have a kind good loving caring heart towards everyone. That way you will feel good about yourself. Other people and you will be able to live a life. Where you will feel peaceful joyful content happy. In harmony at ease within yourself and towards other people.

Maintaining friendships is what holds us together as people. We all like to be listened to especially in times of difficulty. Your friends are a mirror of you as a person. Treat your family and friends with respect and sincerity. People like honesty at all times. It never pays not to speak the truth. If you are like this then people won't have trust in you. Honesty is always the best policy. Always do the right thing by people. When you do the right thing people will do right.

Always be honest and careful with yourself and other people. No matter how another person treats you. If someone is trying to rub you up the wrong way. Be nice and kind and quietly walk away. No one can make you unhappy that's only if you let them. Be happy because you are alive. You have got your health and never let anything or anyone get the better of you. We are forever changing in time with our own personal growth. Look at the challenges you are faced with in positive ways. Challenges make us stronger and more capable. To handle ourselves in the situations we are in. Have faith in yourself. Achieve your goals so you feel satisfied and happy.

Rise above any disappointments that might happen. Don't hold any grudges against anyone. No matter how they mistreat you. Don't let anything ever bring you down. Accept what happens to you. If you experience a disappointment or if you are in a situation. Where your job of relationship with someone doesn't work out. Try and move on very quickly after seeking support and good advice from people you trust. Good things will come your way in time once you do this. Try not to dwell on things. Have productive days. Plan things to look forward to and enjoy and love your life always and forevermore.

When you hang in there with perseverance you will find your strengths of patience courage determination understanding. You will also discover other strong qualities from your own potentials and abilities. Believe in yourself. Don't let set backs get the better of you. Rise above such disappointments and other doors will open in time. We don't know how long we have got to live our lives on this Earth. Make the most of every single day of your life. When you think about it life is short. Fulfill your days with what you enjoy and love doing.

Spend more time with your family and friends and have good times with happiness and laughter. Look forward to every day of your life. You only live once. Any difficulty you experience there is always a way around it with a solution. That will come to you in time. Allow yourself to think through all of the possibilities of your solutions. You can take to overcome your challenges. Always believe in yourself.

Look at this as an enjoyable process. You will see astonishing results this way. You can handle anything that happens to you. There is a way around everything you will ever go through. You just need to give yourself the time to discover the solutions. Of your difficulties on your journey of your life. Look forward to every day of your life. Feel good about who you are. Have respect for yourself and other people. Don't let anyone make you feel unhappy. You have it in you to not let this happen. By taking absolutely no notice of such behaviour. Remember to be kind to those people who you think.

Might be holding any kind of grudges towards you. Remember to love and forgive those people who hurt you always and forever. When you do this you will feel so much better about yourself in your life. Have a wonderful life full of what you enjoy and love doing. Don't let anything get in the way of you achieving your goals. Have the determination and motivation to succeed with fulfilling your desires ambitions dreams. Be proud of your accomplishments. Practice being patient with yourself and other people.

Be open to other people's options. You can take with opportunities that you think. Will be worthwhile that you think will better you as a person. Enjoy everything you do and do it well. Look forward to the wonderful times you have with your family and friends. The small things in our lives that we do make our lives pleasurable. You can achieve anything you have ever wanted to achieve. Anything is possible. To achieve your goals you have to be patient consistent lenient motivated inspired. It takes guts to have a full life.

You can attain this. There are so many beautiful rewards you get from being a motivated and determined person. Never ever give up on anything. Keep on trying to do your very best in your life. You can make your life wonderful. If you want it that way. Don't sit back and wait for things to happen to you. I'll tell you now you will be waiting a long time. Get out there and fulfill your goals. Create a fabulous life for yourself. Full of interesting and fun things to do with your family and friends. The best is yet to come. Make the most of every day.

Start preparing by organising a wonderful career. That you know you are gifted and talented in. That you know you are good at and that you love doing the most. With any goal that you want to achieve. It is important to start off small and then work your way up. To build on your confidence work on knowing what you need to know. On how to improve yourself to achieve. Be good at working towards your target goals. The more time and effort you put into working. At achieving your goals the better you will feel about yourself.

For all of the hard work you have been doing for yourself. It really does pay off in the end. People who know you really well. Like your family and friends can see your achievements. They will support you in every great way. They can help you continue doing well in your life. The key is to find out what you are good at and what you enjoy and love doing the most just go for it. Don't look at your past and regret anything. The only thing that is important about any regrets that you might have made. Is that you have learnt from your mistakes. Start a fresh start accept what has happened to you.

Move into a new and exciting future that is full of how you want it to be like. You can achieve anything that you have ever wanted to achieve. The choice is yours. Look forward to every single day of your life. Never look back just keep moving forward. We all have a purpose here on this Earth. There are reasons why we have been through what we have been through. Our reasons for hardship is so we learn to be stronger and more capable to handle anything that we are faced with. Become self aware and self sufficient. Your attitude in every situation you are in is what will help you to cope.

Nothing in your life will ever be very bad that you can't handle. Although it might seem that way at the time. We are made to cope with everything that happens to us good and bad. We have the choice to accept what has happened. By learning to cope the best way we can. Work on our attitudes in every situation we are put in.

Never ever give up on anything. Keep on striving to do your very best to achieve your goals. Be persistent with your desires of your heart. Until you have reached what you have always wanted to do. Always have hope for better things to come your way. In the right time better things will happen to you. Keep on trying with all that you do always hope for the best. If you do good and mean well then good things will happen to you. Having relationships is what makes our lives worthwhile. We all need someone to love in the good times and bad times. From time to time we all need a shoulder to cry on.

In all relationships it is the friendship that holds both of you together. It is important in any relationship to have trust and compassion towards each other. Having relationships is about sharing listening giving out good advice. Being supportive and understanding from knowing. Where the other person is coming from. By putting yourself in the other persons shoes. Advising them in ways that you think will help them the most. Enjoy every day of your life. The days are yours to do whatever you want to do. Discover your gifts and talents and work in the field. Life is yours.

Have interests and get involved with interests that you are good at and gifted in. Seek encouraging support from your family and friends. Along the way of your discoveries. Look forward to the beginning of each day. Each day is the opening to something new and exciting. Plan to do interesting and fun things in your leisure time. Work hard at finding the right contacts for the beginning of a wonderful career.

Anything is possible. Never ever lose hope in your life. You are precious valuable special important. Have the determination to succeed with your goals. Be ambitious don't let anyone of anything bring you down. You have it in you to have a wonderful life. This life you have is yours and yours to live in anyway you want to. Go for it do what you want to achieve life is short. Love what you do.

Make your life a long and wise life. Each day is a gift. Live your days to the fullest. Plan to do things you enjoy and love doing. With your friends in your leisure time. There will be people you will come across that might be short tempered towards you. It is important to take no notice of such people. Learn to love and forgive these people. Remember there will be more people who will like you. Try to associate with these people more if you can. Avoid those other people who you think aren't sincere towards you. Nobody can make you feel upset because you have the strength and ability to know. That you are a terrific person despite what other people might think of you. Get in touch with your strengths and talents that you have.

Discover what you are good at. Use these strengths in your every day life with your work and at your interests. Don't take any notice of those people who might be critical towards you. At the end of the day the most important thing is how you feel about yourself. With what has happened to you that day. Be proud of yourself for your achievements. Don't worry about what other people might say about you. You have the choice of what kind of quality of life you want to live. You can choose to have a rich life full of what you like and enjoy doing. At your work and your interests. Make your dreams come true

That way you are a person will grow in confidence. You will develop life's coping skills a long the way. By encountering all types of people in the journey of your life. Handle everything that happens to your wisely. Take what you are faced with in your stride. Never let anyone get the better of you. Be happy with who you are. After discovering your strengths gifts talents. Use these more and more in your every day life. At your work and at your interests. Life is wonderful.

Every day work on having the determination to work up to achieving your goals. Be optimistic because you have a bright meaningful truthful fruitful amazing future ahead of yourself. Create an incredible rewarding life for yourself. Be grateful and happy that you are alive. You have got your health your family and your friends. Work will come to you the more you are out there looking for it. Another thing that is important is having interests. You enjoy doing.

Life's too short to be bickering with people. Enjoy your days by doing things you like doing. Be in the company of people who make you feel good. Don't live your life in fear. Have faith that you are going to be okay always. We maybe in the most traumatic times in our lives. This should motivate you to be brave to have courage within yourself. Know that no matter what happens that you are going to be okay. Spend more time with your family and friends enjoy their company. Have faith in God know that life after this life will be such a very better blissful tranquil perfect harmonious peaceful place.

Accept how things are and try to be positive and contented in this world. Although it is not at all easy for any of us. Be with your family and friends. Appreciate them for their support and kindness towards you. The world might seem like a scary place to be in at this point in time. All we can really do is hope and pray for the best. For ourselves and for our family and friends. Fear nothing because God is here. After death there is continuation of life in The Paradise of Heaven with God always and forever to come forevermore. Now's the time to fulfill your desires as we know that life is what you make of it.

For all of us we don't know when we will be taken. We are living in hope to see tomorrow. Always be kind loving good to people. Do good to everyone you come in contact with in your days. Forgive your enemies always do kind and good to people. Show your care and love to your family and friends. Practice loving and forgiving people if you feel hurt by them. Try not to fear because God is with us. God knows all that is going on with us. God will protect us from evil. Have faith in The Lord Jesus Christ. Know that we are in God's capable hands at all times. God will make you loving and just.

Continue praying for what you would like to see happen for yourself in your life. God will make all of your dreams come true especially for you. All in God's right and best time. Learn to really love the person you are. Have the confidence and respect for yourself always. In every situation you are in take the time to really think thoroughly. About what you are setting yourself in for. Never put yourself or anyone in any danger. Your safety always comes first. Always learn from your mistakes. Never make the same mistake again.

Always go with what your gut is telling you. You know what is right and wrong so always listen to God's Wisdom. Take every precaution that is possible to make sure you are safe and okay. Don't take any silly risks ever because you are too precious special valuable important. Look after yourself always look out for yourself and your family and friends. Always mix with a very good circle of people.

We have choices. If you want to be happy and feel good you can. The way you can achieve this is by doing. What you are good at and gifted in. This way a lot of good things come out of your talents with your work and hobbies. As a result of getting involved with what you are good at and gifted in. The astonishing results of feeling content peaceful joyful happy within yourself. You will feel pleased with your own achievements. Then this is brought through to your family and friends. They see this wonderful result you are achieving so continue doing what you enjoy and love doing. What you give out will return.

The person we are to this day. Is from all of our experiences that we have learn't from in our past. Determination comes from our own inner strengths. That we have learn't to develop in our lives. Hope keeps us as human beings going on our own different paths. If you really want a rich life full of wonderful times. To come you can achieve this by being in tune. With what you want to achieve and being aware of people around you such as. Your Employers your fellow co workers. People where you are studying people you are involved with at your interests. God will provide all of your needs.

Respect and be nice to your family and your friends. It is always important to remember to treat people with respect. Even if people don't treat with respect. Always forgive your enemies. Always guard yourself from danger. Follow your instincts with all that you do. We are living is an evil world especially at this time. Shift your focus with thinking positively and being optimistic in your life.

Always do good to yourself and other people. Never lose hope because you have a lot to look forward to in your future.

If you do good to yourself and other people. Then that's what you will attract in your life. Treat people with respect just how you yourself would like to be treated. Be determined to succeed by achieving your goals. Don't let anything or anyone deter you from what you want to achieve. The world is yours to live in any way you wish to. You can accomplish absolutely anything you want. Anything is possible.

Practice being optimistic by hoping for the very best for yourself in your life. It's not at all your problem if someone doesn't like you. They are the one that is missing out getting to know. Such a wonderful person like you. It is their loss not yours. Never put yourself down. Be happy with who you are. Fulfill all of your dreams. Be thankful grateful appreciative that you are alive. Be grateful for everything you have in your life. Never ever lose hope because you have a lot to offer to give people. People are inspired by you always.

Loneliness is what motivates us to get involved with work activities interests. We are much better off when we apply ourselves actively. With work and having interests to go to. When we do this we will feel a lot happier within ourselves and satisfied with our achievements. Start making positive steps into bettering yourself. By getting involved with what you have always longed to become. Discover your qualities that you have and make it an interesting journey for yourself. Achieve all of your heart felt dreams totally.

The path that has been chosen for us is what makes us as human beings unique special important valuable. Don't put yourself down with criticism. Be loving and kind to yourself always. Fill your thoughts up with beautiful lovely good positive thoughts. That will motivate and encourage you to carry on in your life. Don't give up on anything because you are too precious worthy special important.

Try not to be despaired by anything in your life. Hold on to the hope you have to reach the good times that lie ahead of you. Organise things to do that you will look forward to and you will enjoy and love doing. Try not to worry about anything. Work on changing your attitudes towards the things that might be harbouring over you. Believe in yourself always and never ever give up on anything. Never ever lose hope in your life because you have too much going for yourself. Hang in there with all that happens to you. Accept how your life is and work on changing what you think needs to be changed. There is a lot to look forward to in your life. Life is good.

Discover this and always remember to tell yourself positive motivational encouraging inspirational meaningful truthful affirmations. You might feel like you are alone but really when you think about it you aren't. You can choose to get out there and get involved with work and interests that you like and enjoy doing. Make the most of every day of your life. Make the most of the situations you are in in your life. Don't be too hard on yourself if things don't turn out the way you would of liked them to. Be kind to yourself and be kind to other people also. Fulfill your dreams try your very best.

To cope with all that happens to you how you yourself know. Be your best friend. Create and plan a rich career for yourself that you think you can accomplish. Discover what gifts and talents you have and get involved in these areas. This way doors will open for you. When one door closes another door will open. Learn to accept people for how they are. Never judge anyone. What you give out you will get back. Treat people just the way how you yourself would like to be treated.

Succeed with achieving your goals and fulfill your dreams. People will be drawn to when you show them kindness enthusiasm understanding. Sometimes we need to put people before us in some situations. Each of us are special unique important valuable. We are all equal the only difference is is that we have different gifts and talents. Be proud of who you are. Show respect for people who you come in contact with. Be grateful and happy that you are alive.

You have got your health your family and your friends. Work will come to you the more you are out there looking for it. Another thing that is important is having interests. Life's too short to be arguing with anyone. Enjoy and love your days by doing things you like doing. In the company of people who make you feel good content happy. Find ways to help yourself to cope with the struggles that life hands you. Have respect for yourself and have respect for other people you know and who you meet. Try not to lose your cool with people. You will have more control over yourself when you remain calm relaxed.

Even if people are trying to get to you. You don't have to let people get to you. You have the control to ignore such behaviour because you know better. Find inner peace inner joy inner happiness within yourself in moments throughout your days. This is something we all have. When you can get in touch with your inner self you will see what miracles and wonders it will do for you. When people see you happy and doing well. People can see this and they can try to say and do hurtful things towards you. They don't understand why and how you are always happy and they aren't. Happiness comes from within.

When you have a clear understanding of who you are and what your purposes are on this Earth. Your life will then have meaning fulfillment direction joy peace happiness importance inspiration. When you really feel like you are living. You will be filled with laughter enthusiasm joy peace happiness fearlessness courage motivation determination excitement. With what you are driven to the most. At your best with your strengths gifts talents ambitions.

God is a God filled with hope and love. You will never be completely on your own. God is with you in Spirit everywhere you go. God knows how to help you even in the saddest of times. God will always love you no matter what you go through and how you feel. Have Faith in God and God will bless you in your life. Whatever you ask your Father God for. God will listen to your prayers and God will answer your prayers. In God's Perfect and Amazing Timing.

Never lose hope because God loves you. God will continue to love you for the rest of your life here on this Earth. If you believe in God you will join God in The Kingdom of Heaven. When God chooses for you to be with God in Heaven. There won't always be people you can turn to when you are feeling on your own and when you feel lonely. You have to have things you can do that you can turn to in times like this. You are your own boss in your life. You need to find things you can do to fill in your time. Having a job to go to will benefit you a lot in positive ways. Also doing a course of some sort is a very good way.

Off adding to your employment in the long run. Working on having productive things to do in your week. That will help you a lot of ways. It will give you confidence and it will give you a purpose in your life. We all need to feel we have a purpose in our lives. It is important to have structure in your week. The more you are comfortable and content within yourself. When you are able to discover your strengths gifts talents desires. You are then in a better position to be satisfied and happy with your own accomplishments. Life is great.

Have plenty of things in place to do to help yourself to get through the times you have on your own. Make some time in your days to relax. Enjoy being in your own company by doing what you love. Do the things that make you feel good. We learn and grow through our pain and suffering. We all suffer in different ways throughout our days. It is important to have commitments to go to and things to do when you are on your own. Create a fabulous and awesome life.

To distract yourself from how you are feeling. This helps with keeping you occupied. Keep on working on this every day. Find out what you like and enjoy doing do these things more. There will be times where you will feel at a loose end and maybe a bit down. This is a part of how we are made. If we didn't know what it was like to be down we wouldn't appreciate the good times. Life is a long lived adventure. Not everyone will be nice to you in life. Forgive them.

We all have different personalities. For instance a caring person won't connect well with an uncaring person. This has got to do with the way they feel about themselves. The way we feel about ourselves shows through how we treat people. We don't all get on well with everyone in life. There will only be 5 people who we will get on extremely well with in our life time. All the other people will be acquaintances. Stay away from those people who you clash with. Have very little to do with them. Know that what they say to you or about you isn't really that important. Think of the people your best friends. Who like and enjoy being in your company. Who love you.

Support your best friends in the most respectful considerate kind good loving fair ways you know how. When you meet people don't automatically think they will be genuine towards you. People you meet might at first appear nice but in time you will find out their true colours. Don't put all of your trust in people you meet for the first time. If you do you could set yourself up to get hurt. Be wary of people you can't trust everyone. In life you need to know how to stand up for yourself at times. Be assertive when you need to.

You also need to know how to protect yourself from nasty people. Be with the right and best people. Not everyone you meet will come up to your standards. Life is about doing what you like and enjoy doing. We are forever searching for things to do that we find interesting and fun. When choosing a career you have to make sure that you are suited to it. What the job requires and that you have got the strengths gifts talents of the job. Find the right job of your niche.

Have variety in your life. Remember back to what took your interest that you enjoyed doing and do more of these things. Plan your days with what interests you and that you love doing. Explore different activities to do. Work in a field that you are good at and talented in. The way to grow as a person is to get involved with what you are interested in and what you are good at. No person can have any affect on you. If you look at these situations like that person is going through their own issues in their life. All of ourselves are in control.

That explains their negative behaviour towards you. It has nothing to do with you. Remember not to take it personally. You are in charge of your own life. No one else is. Don't wait for things to come to you. Get out there and start to make things to happen for yourself. Contact as many employers that you are happy with and go to for interviews to find work. Expand your social life by getting involved with what interests you as work and hobbies. If you think it's time to study again then apply to do a course. The more things you do the more things you will have to talk about people you will have to meet. The more it will be adding to your own Personal Development. Get out there by making a start to a fantastic amazing great life for yourself. No person can bring you down. You have the ability to not let any one to affect you in any negative way. Be proud of who you are have confidence in yourself. Be what you have always dreamed to become. Make your dreams come true especially for you. Be happy within yourself with all that you do. Rise above the set backs.

Don't give up on anything. Have faith and hope for things to come your way. Learn the gift of patience. Your life is made how you would like it to be. You can change anything you aren't happy with. Have the motivation and determination to do well. Change what you think needs to be changed. Always be happy with who you are. Everything in your life will work out. You will meet that special person in the right time. Remember there is someone out there for all of us.

Look on the bright side of life. Don't be unhappy. Don't be bitter towards anyone it won't make you have a kind good loving heart. Always and forever love your enemies. There is a way around everything you will ever go through. If one thing doesn't work out then something better will work out. You will never be completely on your own. There will always be someone that you will be able to help you. It just takes your thoughts and planning. Ask you shall receive.

Keep your spirits up because you have got a lot ahead of you to look forward to. Nothing will ever be that bad. You can cope with anything and everything that happens to you. Believe this and know this in your heart. Believe in yourself. Know that you have got what it takes to have a wonderful meaningful inspiring rewarding life. Never despair or lose hope. There are good times ahead of you. You can make a terrific life for yourself if you want it to be that way. Remember to forgive those people who hurt you learn to put people before you sometimes. God is full of love and forgiveness. God knows everything about us. God is forever there to hear our words when we are worried and afraid. When we are thankful and happy.

No matter what you go through in your life. God will always be there to listen to us by answering our prayers. God will protect us from evil. Having freedom is what helps us to be independent in our lives. No person has got any kind of control over what we want to do for ourselves not even our parents. As adults we are quite capable of decisions for us because then it doesn't come from you. You know yourself better than anyone so listen to yourself. Seek advice from your friends who you know you can completely trust and confide in.

Learn to structure your time well how you want it to be. Try new activities that you think you might enjoy and love doing. Listen to yourself and expand your options by listening to people who you know and trust. Do something different. Give out compassion kindness goodness love. Always support those people who you care about. What you give out you will get back. Enjoy yourself because you only live once. Teach yourself what makes you the happiest.

Do these things more and more every day of your life. Do what makes you feel good. Be around people who bring you joy peace happiness. We are all important people. Don't do destructive things to yourself. Like who you are. Be kind loving good to yourself always. Fill your mind up with beautiful lovely kind good loving thoughts. Be happy for the times you have on your own. Do interesting and fun activities that you enjoy that makes you happy. Be happy in yourself.

Choose your partner wisely. Make sure your partner has what you are looking for and you both are compatible. Make sure you both have similar interests and you have a lot in common. You know what you like in a person so go by your own judgements. Take the time to really think about what you want with all that you do and go for it. Make the most of every moment. People will come and go from your life. That is a part of being a human being. Some people who you get a long well with will remain. As you do more you will meet people along the way that you will connect with. You can't be close friends with everyone you meet. There is only a few people you be close to.

What we talk about is a reflection about how we feel within ourselves. Don't spend your time worrying about what might happen. Enjoy the present moment always. Get on with what you want to do and achieve. Get involved with what you really love doing the most. Never put yourself down with criticism. Always be kind good loving to yourself. Like who you are and be your own best friend. Have the strength to get through any difficulties that you might be going through. Be prepared for anything that might arise with you. Set yourself the appropriate goals ambitions dreams.

Look at the challenges you are faced with in a positive way. The challenges you go through will empower you by making you a stronger and a more capable person. Discover what you like to do in your time and get involved with these things. Don't be too hard on yourself if things don't go as you planned them to. Never blame anyone for anything. Learn the skill of being assertive when you need to. Don't let anyone get the better of you. You are worth so much.

Don't mix with people who bring you down a lot. If a friend of yours is going through a difficult time. Be there to listen to them don't make their problem yours. Do things that make you feel good inspired uplifted great. Fear nothing you will always be safe. Find a job so you will have structure to your week. Having a job gives you a good opportunity to meet people. You will make new friends.

It also secures you financially. Which is important to all of us so we can pay our own way in our lives. Be happy with how your life is and work hard at improving and bettering who you are any way you wish to. You can overcome any difficulty you are experiencing in your life. Once you know how then it will become easier. Work out the reason to your problems. Like why you are doing whatever it might be. Start by coming up with new ideas and strategies. You can do and take to get over the obstacle you have been struggling with. There is a way and a solution to everything you go through. You just need to know how to go about it. Don't give up trying to work out the solutions.

We all suffer and hurt in our lives. The important thing is how we handle our suffering and hurt. Some people turn to another substance like cigarettes and alcohol. Other people use exercise as a stress release. Eating well by getting the right nutrients and vitamins. Will help you to reduce any kind of stress. Sometimes it is good just to feel the hurt you are going through. Until it passes then you will feel a lot better after you have gone through the pain. Time heals.

You can then choose to let it go by never allowing it to come back. Once you learn the skill of handling your own emotions you will be set to achieve absolutely anything you want in your life. Acknowledge your weaknesses by being aware of them. Work on changing your weaknesses until you start getting positive results. Use your motivation and determination with this. Don't worry about what other people think of you. It isn't important. Love yourself.

It matters how you treat other people and yourself. Don't be nasty to anyone. Have a kind good loving heart. Forgive and love people when they do wrong towards you. Be happy that you are alive. In every bad situation something good will come out of it. Focus your energy on friendships work interests. Practice getting yourself on top of what you go through. Master your work well to the best of your ability. Don't let people bring you down at work or wherever you maybe. Be comfortable being the person you are. Believe in yourself.

Don't judge anyone ever. Accept people for how they are. Do what makes you happy. Always respect people's wishes. Be the boss of your own life. Make your own decisions. Our insecurities and struggles mould us into more courageous people. You can make whatever you want to see happen to you to become your reality. Set yourself goals small and large. Make the steps into achieving your goals ambitions dreams. Seek encouraging support from people you relate well with. Be grateful thankful appreciative for your family and friends. Appreciate them for their support. Don't hold grudges towards anyone. If you really want to do something you will do it.

Never stop trying to defeat your challenges until you get through them. Be consistent motivated determined. Never ever give up. You can change anything in your life that you aren't happy with. Have faith in yourself. Every challenge you get through makes you stronger and more capable. It moulds you into a resourceful person. Live your days with thankfulness and happiness. Be grateful for everything you have in your life. Do a good gesture for someone. When you get through a challenge you are or have been experiencing. Reward yourself by doing something nice for yourself that you like.

It could be putting on some makeup wearing some perfume visiting a friend doing some gardening cleaning up your house reading a book going for a long walk watching a movie doing an enjoyable hobby. Before you do anything think about what you are putting yourself in for. Look after your health. Exercise regularly and eat well. Don't do anything to the excess. Do everything in moderation. Be kind loving good to people. Respect yourself. Do kind deeds for everyone.

Take care of yourself and be proud of who you are. With anything that you go through there will always be a way around your difficulties. Once you get through your difficulties you will see remarkable results of your own strength and capability. Hang in there because in time your life will pick up and improve. Learn how to handle your own emotions. You can do everything and anything.

God knows everything about all of us. God is always very loving and forgiving. God loves all of us. God has a lot install to give us. God created beauty in this world. God is full of love kindness goodness love compassion forgiveness sympathy empathy. God will always protect us from evil. Do the right by God by believing in God always. God loves to hear our prayers. God will answer your prayers in God's Perfect and Amazing Timing. Only you know how to fix your own problems. You know yourself better than anyone. No one else can solve your problems. People can give you advice but in the end only you can fix your problems. Try and stay on top of everything always.

Enjoy every day of your life. God has a plan for all of us. Honour your Father God and all will go well for you. Know that anything you are going through God can and will fix it for us. God is kind good loving forgiving. Believe in God because God is the righteous one. God is our teacher. Without God we wouldn't have kindness goodness love forgiveness compassion sympathy empathy. God wants us to be happy. God will help us to get through our difficulties. When we turn to God and believe in God. God is eternal and everlasting. Gods there

God will always be in The Kingdom of Heaven Forever and ever. God is love. If we believe in God we will join God in Heaven. When God decides when it is our time to be in Heaven with God. You know what you want for yourself so discover this and start to make the steps into achieving your desires. You know who your true friends are. These people accept you for how you are and they won't ever judge you. You can't be close to everyone there are only 5 people who will stick by you and who will be close to you. Friends are rare.

Respect yourself and look after yourself. Look out for the people you care about. There will always be someone who will listen to you. It is just a matter of being persistent and tolerant. Try ringing a great friend. Feel proud of yourself for reaching out. You could be delighted with the outcome. Don't bottle up your emotions. There is no one in the world like yourself there never will be. You are special important unique. You are precious and valuable. Believe in yourself.

The way you feel matters. Learn how to handle your own emotions the best way you can. You are in control of you no one else is. Like who you are. Take what happens to you in your stride. Don't let anyone get the better of you. Be grateful and happy for everything in your life. You are a survivor and you will make it through until the end of your time on this Earth. If you enjoy what you are doing during your days with work and play. Then you can tackle any addiction you have head on. Continue adding activities related to your work life and for fun until you confront your issues completely.

Let go of any hurt from your past and deal with this appropriately by seeking counselling. You will find you will progress this way for the better. Concentrate on how you are at this present moment in time now. Ask yourself are you satisfied and happy with your achievements and what are your future goals. If the answer is yes you must be a competent person who knows where you are headed and what direction you are going in. Knowing and having awareness understanding is the first step into changing the things in your life.

That you know needs to be changed. Once you are able to see beyond all the hurdles from your past. Into a positive light you will feel so much better and you will know that you can handle absolutely anything that comes your way. If you want good things go happen to you. You can achieve this by getting in touch with yourself. By asking yourself what do I like to do that makes me happy. Once you know this there is nothing stopping you from going from smaller goals to bigger goals that you know you can achieve.

If you really want to do something you will find a way to do it. Your determination from within yourself. Will shine through until you have achieved your goals. This could be related to a short or long lived habit. That you feel has become a big part of your life. You can take small positive steps into breaking whatever it maybe so start now into creating a full life of what you want it to be like. It doesn't matter at all what people think of you. Rise above people's cruelty.

Have confidence and pride with who you are. Be proud of your achievements. Don't let yourself be brought down by any kind of negativity. Block this out and say something positive. We are what we think of ourselves and other people. Try and look at your experiences in an optimistic way. Get in touch with the part of you that is driven to become successful for yourself. Once you do this there will be nothing stopping you from going from strength to strength. Achieving absolutely anything you could possibly ever want. Hold on to the hope you have to get through what faces you.

Never ever give up. Have the strength to handle anything that comes your way. Don't be afraid of anything. Have faith that everything will be okay. Do what sparks your interest. Don't live your life in fear. Always live your life in God's unconditional love. Be brave and have the courage to continue doing what makes you happy. Your life is here to be enjoyed so figure out what you like doing and make these things your weekly routine. Work out what you would like to change in your life and start making positive steps into changing these things. Think of ideas that will help you into making these changes.

You can replace your old habits with new healthy and positive habits. That won't be so detrimental to yourself. Discover what you would be interested in adding to your weekly schedule and go for it. In time you will mature and become wiser. The challenges that you have been put in your life have been put there for a reason. To make you stronger and more capable to handle more that will arise with you. Challenges aren't a bad thing. Look at your challenges in a positive way. Like they are moulding you into the person you are to this day.

You can stop any addiction you have been struggling with. If you take the right steps that work for you. What you tell yourself is the first step then exercising as much as you can. Having a job and doing what interests you. It also helps to have support with this from your family and friends. Find as many things you can do that will help you to overcome your addictions. Everyone suffers in some way in life.

Having a positive attitude is a big bonus. God is full of kindness goodness love. You can see how God has worked wonders for you in your life. God has blessed you. God will continue to bless you and reward you forever and ever. On Earth and in The Kingdom of Heaven For All Of Eternity. Give thanks to your Father God in Heaven because God is your provider. Believe in God and you will see how your life will change for the better. Remember to Honour your family when you need to. Forgive them for their unfair treating's if this is the case. You don't need any kind of crutch in your life. Life is good.

If you are feeling worried or unsure about something there is no need to turn to an unhealthy substance. It won't make you feel better. It will make you feel worse than you already were so have a healthy lifestyle. Work on taking as many healthy and positive steps into being free from any kind of addiction that has been a part of your life. For a short length of time or long length of time. You can succeed in changing this. If you really want to so believe you can do this and know you can achieve this. With God everything is possible.

Choose something in your life that you aren't happy with. Think of how you can make steps into changing these negative habits. If you really want to change an old habit that has been in your life for a long time you can. Once you try as many small and different strategies to help you to get through. If you never ever give up you will win all of your impossible battles. Anything is possible if you really want it. Get your mind off yourself by doing something productive. Be resourceful eventful show initiative eagerness.

It could be going to work, reading an interesting book, going for a walk and breathing in the fresh air, going for a swim, working out at the gym. If you are unemployed then apply for work. Find out what you yourself like and enjoy doing. In time you will find you will be a lot more satisfied and happier. Not everyone of the opposite sex will have what you are looking for. Don't let this get you down.

Accept this and move on. Be clear with what your needs are. Someone who will be even more compatible and special will come along and will make you even more happier. There is someone out there who you will meet all of your needs. All in the right and best ways. When it is meant to happen remember this. Don't worry what other people think of you it doesn't matter at all. What other people think of you. You know who your true friends are. Don't surround yourself with negative people you don't need this. Surround yourself with people who want the best for you who make you feel satisfied and happy. If someone has upset you don't rush back to them.

Straight away take the time to think if you really want this person to be your friend. Not everyone will be suited for your friendship. Peoples different sides can show when you really get to know them. You can decide which people you like with their qualities attributes characteristics. You can get through any emotional difficulty you are experiencing. Once you are aware of what your concern is. You can take steps for yourself to overcome your concerns. Life's about hope.

Try and look on the positive side of your challenges deal with your challenges appropriately. Even if it means talking through your concerns. With the person you have come in conflict with. You will feel so much better about yourself. Once you talk your concerns with the person who is involved. Never ever give up. You are the only one who knows your difficulties the best. We all struggle from time to time about something in our lives. It could be a relationship breakup, dealing with loneliness, loss of a job the list goes on. Believe in you.

You need to have coping strategies to help you to survive the challenges you are faced with. Life isn't always easy. It is hope that helps us to keep on going. Think of what you like doing that makes you excited and happy. Do more of these things and you will start seeing the positive benefits of your achievements. Remember that it is easy for other people. To say hurtful things when they themselves. Are going through something stressful in their own lives. Forgive.

Don't have fears of your death. Know that after this life you will be in The Paradise of Heaven. If you believe God. Your prayers will be heard by God. Your prayers will be answered in God's Perfect and Amazing Timing. Forgive your enemies. Be kind loving good to your family and friends. Do something kind and thoughtful for your family and friends. They deserve this because they really care about you. Your past experiences have moulded you into the person you are to this day. If you have ever experienced a crisis in your life. Which all of us do at some stage. You will find that something good will come out of it. Rise above your insecurities in appropriate ways. Be happy.

Always learn from your mistakes. You have the potential and capability to get over any difficult challenge. Once you know how to apply yourself. Be determined motivated consistent. By using your strengths and abilities to meet your goals. You can do absolutely anything you want. Having motivation determination consistency. Are the three major attributes of achieving success of any kind you like. It doesn't matter at all what people think of you. Love yourself.

It only matters what you think about yourself. You come first then other people in your life come second. If someone is critical towards you take no notice. Know that you are a good person despite what they might think and say. Be kind to yourself like who you are. Remember if people are being critical towards you. It is because they are not happy within themselves try and understand this. Let it go.

Don't let anyone bring you down. Rise above this when you need to put people in their place. In an assertive way do it in a calm firm and a well controlled way. Don't let anything bring down. Be glad and happy with how things are going for yourself. Appreciate your family and friends. They care about you and they are interested in you. They only want the best for you. Do a nice gesture for someone you care about it could be anything special. Discover what makes people satisfied and happy. Do these things more often for them. Be happy.

Always be kind good loving to the people you love the most. Get in touch with what you like to do. You know what interests you so start by getting involved with work, study and activities that you like and enjoy doing the most. Join groups of your choice. Get out there and get on with it. Make all of your dreams come true. Don't wait for things to come to you. Get out there and make things happen for yourself. You will be amazed to see what potential you have when you make these steps. Be optimistic not pessimistic. Having determination is what helps you to succeed with achieving your goals. Never lose hope because things will never be that hard.

You can't handle every day be motivated to achieve your desires. Fill your mind up with positive thoughts about yourself and other people. Don't go out of your way to be nasty to anyone. Always be kind to yourself and other people. What you give out you will get back. Always have a kind loving good caring heart. If someone who is close to you says something you find hurtful. Let it wash over you.

After seeking support from a genuine sincere honest trustworthy friend you trust. Sometimes you will find that you can relate on a better level. With your friends rather than your family. This is because your family know you so well. Friends know you better. Your family can say what they think regardless of your feelings. This is called love. Sometimes the people we care about the most hurt us the most. Forgive your family for the pain they have caused you.

They are not perfect no one is well not yet. We all suffer in some way. It is how you deal and cope with your suffering. That makes you into a stronger more motivated resilient determined person. Learn not to let people affect you badly. Be strong and courageous within yourself. Have the stamina to continue to handle the hurdles that arise with you. Never give up and never lose hope. Things will look up for you. You will feel better in good time. Be happy within yourself. Try your very best to remain content within yourself.

Be grateful for everything you have in your life. Honour and respect your family. Try to do right by them. Take the time to think about the consequences to your actions before you make decisions. Forgive your family for their unfairness towards you. Learn how to handle your parents and siblings. With their own set ways of how they cope in their own ways. Master how to maintain relationships with your family. Put them first at times. Think of your family. Don't be selfish always be unselfish. Honour your parents and all will go well with you in the land. Remember this and live by this. It is good for your own Personal Development. Don't be afraid of anything in your life that could happen. Have Jesus Christ Almighty in your life always.

Know that after this life there will be no more pain and suffering. If you believe in God you will be with your Father God Almighty in The Kingdom of Heaven. Where God will make your Spirit Perfect in God's Image. You won't feel pain anymore and you won't suffer anymore. Have courage and determination to cope with life's difficulties that you are faced with. Know that everyone suffers and you will never be perfect here on this Earth. You will always have challenges to get through. No one is perfect. We all make mistakes.

Remember to be as positive as you can in your life. That way you will see your positive achievements. That you yourself have worked so hard at maintaining. Hang in there you will feel better you will progress over time. Be grateful and thankful for the challenges you have in your life. The challenges you go through are making you stronger more forgiving loving capable driven. If someone brings you down hold your head up high. Know that you are a valuable and a worthwhile person who has a lot to offer the world. Love yourself.

Don't give anyone the power to destroy your own happiness. Rise above this negativity. Treat people well with thoughtfulness. Don't be cruel to anyone even if you are hurting in your own life. Always be kind and be assertive when it is appropriate. Coming from a dysfunctional family is common. The way to handle difficult people in your family is to have less contact with them. Try not to let their critical comments affect you. By knowing you are a great person despite what they might say and think of you. Believe in yourself.

At the end of the day you are the one that has to be happy with what you have achieved for that day. It doesn't matter what other people think of you. Respect yourself and look after yourself. Concentrate your energy on working towards achieving your goals. Don't let yourself get brought down by anyone. You are worth so more than this. Pick yourself up as quickly as you can after going through any kind of testing and challenging time. You can get through absolutely anything that will happen to you. Have faith in yourself love yourself.

Never let yourself spiral right down. Practice picking yourself up quickly after going through any difficult time. At times we are all experiencing being on a tough road at different times at different stages of our lives. It is important to remind yourself of your positive achievements. That you are doing or that you have done. We have to go down to get up again sometimes. The more times you get through your struggles the more you will know what to expect the next time around. Have the strength to get through. Always stay positive.

Stay away from negative and critical people. You don't need people like this in your life. It will only destroy your inner tranquillity joy peace happiness. Be at peace. Remember to have less contact with negative and critical people. Always be around people who are positive who encourage you in your life. Who won't create such turmoil and destruction towards you. Also remember to love and forgive the people who hurt you. That way you won't have any bitterness in your heart towards other people like your friends.

When you love and forgive people who mistreat you badly. Then God will love and forgive you. Don't hold onto dislike towards anyone it will only make you unhappy. People won't want to be around you if you are unhappy. Always love and forgive your enemies. If someone is nasty to you don't be nasty back to them. Never sink down to their level of cruelty because it isn't at all good for you. Always be nice.

It will only make you feel bad. Have the wisdom to be respectful considerate kind loving good to your family and friends. Don't speak badly about anyone. What comes out of your mouth will come back to you. If you give out positivity kindness goodness love. Then that's what you will receive in return. Be good by treating people with respect and thoughtfulness even if they aren't treating you in these ways in return. Treat people how you yourself would like to be treated. Remember to live by this. The difficult people who are in your life. Have been put in your life for a reason. To make you stronger and more able to learn how you can handle difficult people.

When you are in a work environment when you are working with someone. Who you find difficult you will be able to handle. These kinds of people a lot easier because you will know how to cope a lot better. You won't let these people affect you because you already know how not to let them bother you. Be grateful and thankful for the difficult people in your life. In time you will see why and how these difficult people. Have changed you into a more resilient motivated capable person. In life it is how you react to people's.

Opinions of you and other people that either makes you a tolerant or an intolerant person. Learning not to react to criticism that is directed towards you is a great skill to have. It is important to work at this every day. If someone says something you find hurtful. Don't be hurtful to them in return. Forgive them. Know the reason why they are being this way towards you. Is because they are experiencing pain and suffering. In their own lives. Don't take offense

You just might be the person at the time who they decide to unload their baggage onto at the time. Try not to take it personally. Try to understand where they are coming from. Always forgive and love people who hurt you. Get in touch with what is making you unhappy in your life. Start making steps into changing these things. Anything you get though in your life. No matter what it is large or small.

You will feel so much better when you get through these hurdles. Every day is a new beginning with new hurdles to get through. Have the determination and persistence to get through by reaching the light at the end of the tunnel. Don't dwell on negative things. Dwell on all of the positive things in your life. Every day that will help you to get through productively and successfully. In time you will heal from all of the traumas. You have been through in your past. You will know how you don't want to be. Take a minute to look at yourself to see how far you have come. You have strengthened with a lot of different qualities of your personality. You have grown and matured tremendously. You have survived with everything you have been.

Through you have turned into a complete and compassionate person. Remind yourself of your wonderful progress. Know that you can and you will be able to handle absolutely anything and everything that comes your way in your life. Remember people make mistakes like you do even your family do. When you are able to forgive people who hurt you. By standing up for yourself in a calm and appropriate way. Send out good and positive words to comfort them from their sorrows. You will start seeing astonishing results. Know they are suffering with something themselves in their lives.

Always do the right thing by being calm and in control of your intentions towards people. Disasters happen because we live in a fallen world. Sometimes disasters happen as a wake up call from God to us as human beings. Honour your Father God in Heaven give your Father God praise and thanks. For giving you this wonderful gift of life God has given you. Give thanks to your Father God for the people in your life. You are on this Earth for a reason. To learn how to forgive and love those people who have hurt you. Love everyone.

You are here to meet those special people who will be your lifelong friends. Who will stick by you through the thick and the thin. Create your own life away from your family with work, study, interests and friendships. One day you will meet that special person who you will connect very well with. In the right and best time when it is meant to happen. Have faith and hope for everything to get better in time. Believe in the power and wisdom of God within yourself and people.

There are good times ahead of you always remember this. With anyone no matter what they say to you even if it is cruel. Know their words aren't at all true. You know yourself the best. What you think of yourself is a lot more important than what other people say about you. Rise above any kind of negativity you think might intentionally be directed at you. People are like this because they are unhappy. With themselves in their own lives. They are taking their problems out on you. Don't let anyone make you unhappy. Forgive them.

Have a break from these people. Time heals all wounds. Your friends will be the ones who will help you to get through everything in your life. Always deal with the pain of your past in helpful and beneficial ways. Have a positive attitude in the present moment. That will help you to cope the most. Discover by working out coping strategies to help you to get through. Never ever give up. Try not to let your difficulties overwhelm you. Believe in yourself. Don't be discouraged about anything in your life. Have hope for a wonderful future that lies ahead of you. You are the boss of your own life no one else is.

Things will never be that bad that you can't handle what you are going through. Use all of your coping resources to get through. Be around people who make you feel good. Learn how to get on with difficult people. There is a way around everything you go through. It just takes your time and intelligence and thinking in appropriate ways. To get through your difficulties. Hang in there with everything you go through. You are important precious special valuable. Despite what other people might think of you. Have a healthy self image.

Concentrate on your goals with what you yourself would like to achieve. Don't let anyone get the better of you. Stand up for yourself appropriately when you need to. Try to look on the bright side of things in your life. Be thankful grateful appreciative for the challenges you go through. With every negative thought you have replace it with a positive thought. Think positively all the time.

Focus on peoples strong points not their faults. Be kind and grateful for the people you care about and love. Don't go out of your way to be nasty to anyone. Accept people for how they are. Continue on the path of your journey in your life. Good things will happen to you in the right and best time when you least expect it. You will meet that special person when you are not looking for them. When it is meant to happen. When you are able to channel your thoughts in a positive light with your life experiences you go through in your life. You are then giving yourself the opportunity to be joyful peaceful happier.

There is power in changing your life with positive thinking. When you are positive everything will improve by getting better and better. Your positive efforts in your life you give to yourself and other people who you care about and love. Will pay off so much to your own advantage. Think of other people who you care about and love more. Focus on their needs you will see what wonders this will do for yourself. Treat people with respect and kindness all of the time. This will come back to you and you will reap the rewards. Karma is there.

Express the beauty from within your heart towards people who you care about and love. To people who you come across throughout the days too. Don't hold grudges towards anyone. Forgive those people that fumble. Don't take peoples words to heart. Learn to be light hearted and don't take people too seriously. You've got to go through the bad to get to the good. If we didn't have bad times then we wouldn't appreciate the good times so much. Be level headed.

Work on what works for you that helps you to cope when you are experiencing anything tough. Remind yourself there are good times ahead of you to look forward to. Be thankful for everything in your life even for the bad things you go through. If we didn't have bad times then we wouldn't appreciate the good times so much. Work on what works for you that helps you to cope when you are experiencing anything tough. Your life will improve and get better.

Remind yourself there are good times ahead of you to look forward to. Be thankful for everything in your life even the bad things. When you are able to do this your life will change for the better. Don't put yourself down instead lift yourself up by telling yourself positive things about yourself. All of the good things you have done and you are doing. Do as many positive things as you can that way. When the hard times come you will look back and remember how good you felt when you did these things. Be motivated to do well for your own well being and your success. The way to excel in your life is by having support from your family and friends. If you give out kindness.

By showing good intentions to people. That's what you will receive in return from other people. Be thoughtful show those people who you care about who you love who you are close to that you care. If you fail at anything in your life. Try try try again until you achieve your goals. Never ever give up don't despair. Have determination to get back on your feet again. Continue trying to achieve your goals until you make it by getting through everything. Those people who stick at their goals those people. Who show persistence and determination will be the ones who will go along way in life. You will be the winner.

When you are useful and helpful this is a bonus. With every negative experience you go through something positive will come out of it. Don't dwell on the worst things in your life for long lengths of times. When you find yourself doing this switch your thoughts into focusing on all of the positive things you have in your life. Remind yourself of all the good memories you have. You have to go through the bad to get to the good sometimes. Good things happen to those people who wait. Concentrate your focus on achieving your goals always.

Spend time with people who enjoy being in your company. Try your very best to continue achieving your goals. Be happy to try not to spend too much time worrying about unnecessary things. Get out there get involved in something that interests you. You can overcome any major obstacle you are struggling with. Make it a thing of the past. Once you use your courage and determination. You can.

Until you conquer your challenges. You will be amazed to see the astonishing results of all of your works. Look at any experience you go through as an experience of the present moment to learn from. Be happy being the person you are. With what you have planned coming up for yourself soon with your goals ambitions aspirations dreams. Always learn from your mistakes. Don't beat yourself up too much. If you make the same mistake again and again and again. None of us are perfect. Look at your mistakes as a learning curve . Give yourself the chance to know that eventually you will learn.

From your mistakes when you are able to be thoughtful and rational. Don't give yourself a hard time over this. Accept that you aren't perfect. Know that you will make mistakes in your future. Just make sure you learn from them. We are made to cope as human beings even through the hard stuff we experience. The more you practice trying to rise above the disappointments that happen to you. When they happen to you the further you will go and learn from that experience. Try not to dwell on the negatives. Be grateful you are alive on this day today. Life is what you make of it. Stay positive.

If you want to be happy and this is how you have chosen. To be in your life then that's how you will be. The way to be happy is to find out what you enjoy doing the most. With what interests you with work, study and your interests. Don't think of the worst instead challenge your focus on what you have to gain. With what you have going for yourself. People will be drawn to you when you are positive happy and content within yourself. You are the master in your life no one else is. What you want will come to you all in the right time.

When it is destined to happen to you. Continue learning from the challenges you go through by being strong bold daring courageous. We all sometimes might think of the worst that is human. When you are able to clarify your fears with someone it won't seem that bad. Like the person you are. Have pride and self respect for yourself. Be your own best friend. Enjoy your own company. One of the most important things in life is to have independence. Always be happy.

Don't spend your time worrying about what could happen. Instead think of what you have got to be grateful for in this day. Make the most of what you have got. Get to know yourself well by enjoying your own company doing what interests you. Discover what gifts and talents you have and do these things every day. None of us know when our time is up. This should motivate you to enjoy your days. Appreciate your challenges and all of the positive things in your life.

Remind yourself about all of the positive things you have in your life. You have the choice and control not to let yourself stay down for too long after experiencing any kind of disappointment. Look on the bright side of things. Look at all the things you have achieved in your life. The people you have met and the experiences you have had and the places you have been. There is so much to look forward to in life it is just a matter of finding our what makes you happy and what you enjoy doing. Go for it with all of your might. Fulfill your desires have fun along the way in the journey of your life. Lift yourself out of the down times you experience. With practice and hard work into.

Changing your outlook into positive thinking. You will see how far you will excel and succeed in your life. When you think about it life really isn't that bad. If you have structure to your week. With things to look forward to with people who you like being around. What more could you want. Any negative experience you go through good things will come out of it. Have hope for things to improve in your life. Every challenge you get through something positive will come out of it. Every challenge you experience is special because it will.

Help you to advance more by learning growing and maturing. You have a lot to look forward to in your life. Every day of your life is special and important. You have gained experience and knowledge with all of the things you have done. Make your mind up to achieve your goals. Achieving your goals is as hard as you make it out to be.

Be ambitious driven and determined to follow through with what you have got install. A lot of good things will come out of your persistence. It will pay off very well after you have achieved your desires. You will know who is the right person for you when you met them. They won't just be any ordinary person. They will be special valuable precious important to you. They will have the same qualities that you are looking for. You will know who will be the right person. With how you both relate to each other the way you both connect.

Have dreams to work towards by making steps into fulfilling your dreams until they come true. Usually what we worry about doesn't become real. Teach yourself to get on top of your worries. To nip your insecurities and doubts in the bud. Before they go to a too far extreme of thinking of the worst. You are the master of your life. You have the control and power within yourself to stop spending your time worrying. Worrying is bad for you. Concentrate on getting in tune with your positive side. By doing as many positive things as you can. That way you will start seeing what potential you have.

With your power of positive thinking. Practice this every day by making it a habit. It takes 21 times to form a new habit. You can teach yourself new skills of being positive renewed and enlightened in your mind always. You just need to get in touch with what will help you to be in this state. Never ever give up on anything. Eventually you will achieve your goals. Try you will succeed.

It doesn't matter how long it takes. Look at all that you are learning in the process. Think of yourself as a winner and that's what you will be. Never compare yourself with anyone we are all different. We all do things at our own individual pace. Be as determined as you need to be to get where you want to be. Do what you have always dreamed of doing. Believe you can do absolutely anything.

You could possibly want once you put your mind to it. Find out what makes you feel good and do more of these things. Know that you have got the potential and ability to do absolutely anything you have always dreamed of. Make your dreams become your reality. Believe in yourself don't let anything bring you down. You have the choice not to be this way. Listen to yourself and do what you know is right for you. You know yourself the best better than anyone knows you. No one else can make your decisions for you. People can advise you but in the end you are the one who decides what decisions you will make for yourself. No matter how anyone acts towards you. You have the choice with how you choose to respond. Be independent.

Don't let anything you are working towards dishearten you if you don't succeed at first. Don't give up until you have achieved your goals no matter how long it takes for you. It doesn't really matter how long it takes you. It doesn't matter just as long as you eventually keep on persisting until you have achieved your goals. Use your persistence and determination in achieving wherever you want. Never ever give up. You will win all of your impossible battles. If you find someone says something to you that you find discouraging.

Don't let it bother you at all. Know that that is there problem not yours. Know that you are a good person and you like how you are so what's the big deal. No one can bring you down that's only if you allow this to happen. You have the choice to ignore such pessimistic words. By making the decision to concentrate on what makes you happy. Know you are a good person who means well who has a lot to offer people and to give in this world. Get in touch with your positive side of yourself. Work out what you think are your strengths gifts use these talents. At work study and at your choice of your interests.

If something doesn't go how you would of liked it to go. Don't let it deter you or make you unhappy. Accept how things turned out in that situation. Maybe it wasn't meant to turn out for a reason. Something better will work out in time that is meant to work out for you. Have hope for the wonderfulness that all of us have. That is the gift of life from The Lord Jesus Christ Almighty. Life is a blessing.

God has put difficult people and challenging situations in your life so you can develop a strong faith love hope in God. God loves to hear your prayers. Believe in your Father God in Heaven. Always forgive and love those people who hurt you. Pray a kind good loving prayer for them. Without God we wouldn't have this beautiful gift of life. Look around at all of the beauty that God has created for all of us here on this Earth. God is full of compassion sympathy empathy kindness goodness love. God is always forgiving. Honour your Father God all will go well for you. God will always be with you forever.

Limit your time with people who are negative and who you feel frustrate you. You are number one so start making steps by surrounding yourself. With people who are positive towards you who always encourage you. No matter how negative or patronizing someone is towards you. Don't let people like this bother you at all. Know that you are a wonderful person who is well liked by people in your life. Don't take on other peoples negativity when they are inflicting their unhappiness onto you. Be kind good loving to people.

Know that you are a very capable person who has so much to give and offer people in this world. No one can make you unhappy that's only if you give them the power to do this to you.

Hold your head up high and trust your own judgements. With all that you do because you know yourself better than anyone will ever know you. This will always be true with what you go through in your lifetime. God will provide you with all you need in your life. God always will. God looks out for each and everyone of us. You can see Gods love reflected.

Through us as human beings. Praise your Father God Almighty. God will bless you and reward you abundantly. Know that God is there to hear your prayers. No matter how small or great they might be. Forgive and love people when you feel hurt by their words. Develop a strong faith in your Lord Jesus Christ Almighty. Your Father God who you will be with one day in The Kingdom of Heaven for all of Eternity. In life it is all about doing things in moderation by being balanced. Be kind to yourself. Create healthy habits every day.

It is important to have plenty of fruit lean meat and vegetables every day. As often as you can especially fruit and vegetables. This gives you your source of energy and vitamins. To maintain your health. When you can eliminate eating fatty foods so much. Start by eating plenty of fruit lean meat like steak and chicken salad vegetables low fat dairy products and nuts occasionally. You will see how much better you will feel both mentally and physically. Having a healthy diet is the most vital part as you as a human being can ever do.

There's nothing wrong with concentrating on your goals with what you want to achieve and being single in the process. It takes time to meet someone who will be compatible for you. Who will meet your needs just how you like it. Once you are able to be peaceful joyful happy. Within yourself doing all of the things you do. Continuing to have great times with your family and friends. Other people you meet can see your positivity joy peace happiness. They will automatically want to be around you.

People will be attracted to your get up and go with how you are a positive and a happy person.

Don't be envious of other people who are getting married and falling pregnant. One day this will be you with absolutely any doubt. That's if you want this for yourself. Be content and happy with how you are. Accept yourself just as you are. Treat your family and friends how you would like to be treated. With kindness respect thoughtfulness. Learn how to handle any difficult person. That is in your life in appropriate ways that suits you the best. Try try you will succeed.

You will develop better coping strategies in time when you grow and mature into a very capable adult. Don't let anyone or anything bring you down. Use your intelligence and positive abilities to overcome. Such discouraging opinions from other people if or when this is the case. Live in the present moment. When you think about it the present moment is all that we have. Head towards an exciting future that is ahead of you. Anything you want to happen in your life.

If you are prepared to work at your ideal desires. Try to work at being optimistic by looking on the bright side of everything. This way you will feel a lot better. Don't take any notice of any back stabbing you predict is happening with people. Stay away from this cruel and inappropriate behaviour. Don't spend your time being part of this unfair and unjust behaviour. People like this are insecure and unhappy within themselves. They think it gives them a kick to their ego acting this way. Make sure you don't be this way you know how to behave. In a lot more kinder and sensible ways. Be nice always.

Never sink down to their levels of cruelty. We are all responsible and accountable for our own intentions and actions. This life we have is a gift and blessing from God. We are all special unique valuable important precious to God. You will connect well with only a hand full of people in your life. You can't be close to everyone. Make what you want to achieve your main focus by seeing your family and friends. Eventually that special person who you are destined to meet will come into your life when you least expect it. Who will be right.

Music is important for our souls and our well being. Music brings joy and happiness to our hearts and souls. Music helps us to appreciate where we are at in our lives. Music brings us hope that there will be someone who. Will be special who will meet your needs in the right time. When it is meant to happen. Hold onto all of your hope you have to fulfill your desires and your dreams of your heart and soul.

Like the person who you are. Be happy in your own company. Doing the things you enjoy doing the most. When you think about it our lives go quite quickly when you look back. This should encourage you to start making plans. For you to get involved with all of the things you have always wanted to do and be. When you think about it things really aren't that bad. Life is what you make of it. Accept what happens to you in your life. Things that turn out are meant to turn out. Things that don't turn out aren't meant to be. Teach yourself to rise above the disappointments that happen to you. The sooner.

You can overcome your challenges with a positive outlook. The better you will feel and the further you will go in your life. Handle all that happens to you calmly and maturely. You will find you will have more control over yourself this way. If you think you don't connect with someone very well in your life. Don't try and connect with them. They will just upset you by making you feel sad. To avoid this happening it is best for you. To concentrate on your goals with work study and doing activities that make you happy. By doing these things you will meet people along the way of your destinations.

You will meet people who you will relate very well with. The people you will meet will be able to relate very well to you. They most probably would have had similar life experiences like you have had. Don't contact people who are getting their kicks out of belittling you. Who you know how they can press your buttons. You are worth so much more than this. Stay away from such cruel people like this. Have a wonderful life of your own you have a lot to look forward to.

Be around people who let you be yourself who care about you. Who are interested in your life experiences. When you are able to relate to people like your friends at all levels of your experiences. You will be amazed at how much better you will feel and how much you will grow and advance as a person of maturity and wisdom. Be guided with what you yourself want in your life. You know yourself better than anyone knows you. This will always be the case throughout your whole life. You are a unique individual with so much to learn in your.

Life from your own experiences and from other peoples. Continue to respect and value yourself every day of your life. Don't take any notice of anyone else's unfair and unjust behaviour you are seeing. Know that they are struggling and know that they have got their own problems. This explains why they are like the ways they are. Know that this is not your problem. This is their own stuff with their own hurt and pain they are experiencing in their life. Don't hurt anyone.

Try not to take it personally. They are the ones that are having trouble communicating appropriately. If someone is coming across in a short and abrupt way. Don't take this on board and make it become your problem. This is not at all your problem. This is their own problem. People like this are insecure and they have got major problems going on in themselves in their own lives. You are not the problem. They are like this because this is how they only know how to cope with the struggles that they are facing. We are forever changing in every precious day of our lives. As we get older we learn grow and mature at our own unique and individual experiences.

Our days that have been given to us are ours to do whatever we please. The days we have are here to be enjoyed and shared with our family and friends. Life is too short to be bickering. Stay away from people like this. Be around people who lift you up who bring you into fulfillment and happiness. People like this do exist. We all see different peoples personalities in our own distinct ways. As we are all different and unique we will get on with some people better than others. Our generational make up makes us the people we are.

We all choose how and what we want to be like from our past experiences. One of the most important things in life is to learn from your mistakes. When we do this we will feel better about ourselves. In control and we don't have as many regrets the next time around. Learning is most important and the major tool in life. Make the time to reflect over the experiences you have been through in your life.

Work out how these experiences have taught you to be the strong and courageous person you are to this day. Hold onto what you want to see happen to yourself in your future. What you want to see happen to you will happen when it is meant to in the right time. Never lose sight of this. You have a lot of interesting and exciting times ahead of you. Accepting how things are in the situations that happen to you in your life. Is the first major step of improving. Yourself into a positive future that is ahead of you. Be positive.

When you are able to look at the circumstances that happen to you. In an accepting and realistic way. You will find how much further you will develop. In confidence maturity and wisdom. Live every day of your life as if it were your last. When you think about it life does go by quickly. Do all of the things you have always wanted to do. Having a full life and doing what you enjoy doing will help you to be happy. It will add for yourself to hold onto a positive attitude even in the most disappointing times. When you can practice being positive especially in the disheartening times. You will discover the strength you have within yourself to handle absolutely any situation that.

You will be faced with in your life. Someone special will enter into your life when this is destined to happen all in the right time. Don't go looking for someone. Usually the way a relationship will last is when it is not rushed and sought. When you are in a relaxed state and when you are yourself with people who know you very well. When you are going along to your work and interests that you enjoy. Not even thinking about meeting anyone. This is more likely when you most probably will meet someone. When you least expect it.

Hold onto the hope you have to survive life's challenges. Look at what you are faced with as a learning curve and an additive to your growth as a person. Hang in there with all that happens to you and try and find out what helps you to cope in your life. In time things will improve and you will feel better about yourself. Try not to think of the worst. Instead plan things to look forward to. You will see how much better you will feel. There are good times around the corner.

Hold onto this thought. Feeling lonely motivates you to get involved with work and your interests. Start making positive steps into getting involved with what sparks your interests. Find the right people to talk to. Into entering the beginning of something interesting and exciting. Think of the people you will meet in the process. You will make new friends and you will do things you have never done before with these people. Make the positive steps and you will feel great and fabulous.

Take the time to distress from your own emotions by doing something productive to get your mind off how you are feeling for a while. Think of other people and do something kind for someone. It could be a small thing. When you do this you will find how much this will change your attitude. The person you have helped will be much appreciated from your kind gesture. Some people will come and go out of your life. This is why it is important to get to know yourself well and like being the person who you are. When you can rely on yourself first and use all of the resources you know to help you cope even in the most crucial times. You will be amazed to discover the.

Strength you have within yourself to get through the hurdles that lye ahead of you. Getting through any challenge that arises with you is a very rewarding experience. You have done it all yourself even when it hasn't been easy. Have the tools behind you to help you to cope even in the toughest of times. Leave all of the pain from your past behind you and make new beginnings for the new positive you. Do what you like to do the most out of all you have tried and even try doing new and fun interesting work and activities. Don't give up.

There are so many opportunities for you to take in your life. When you are able to hang in there and find ways to relax. It is important to find out ways to help yourself to keep your stress levels down. In the most difficult times. Discover what will help you to cope in your life. Plan things that you will look forward to. You will feel better in time with the different experiences that will happen to you. You will get stronger and you will develop more resourceful coping strategies all in good time. Prepare yourself for the hurdles that life hands you.

When you feel low do something that will make you feel better. It could be going for a walk seeing a movie contacting a friend attending a dance class and the list goes on. In life there are things you can do to make you feel better and happy. You just need to discover these things. Make it an enjoyable process. Don't be around people who are negative and critical of you. This is not good for you. It will only make you unhappy and upset. You don't want this and you don't need this to be the way. Don't contact people like this.

Be around people who encourage you with all that you do and who are positive towards you. Who want the best for you in your life. Rise above the difficulties you have in your life. Don't let any person bring you down. Don't give anyone the power to make you unhappy. Be aware there are people in this world who are like this. Even your own family might be like this. Have your own life away from your family if you find them to be negative and critical. You will be a lot happier getting on with what you want to achieve in your life. Life is good.

Without such destructive people trying to control you. Concentrate on doing positive things to help you to survive in your life. This life you have is for you to live in any way you wish to. You have choices and decisions to make with your career and recreational activities. That you and only you really know what you want to do the most. Never ever give up or lose hope. No matter what you are going through. You have so much to live for and get on with. Life's good.

Work towards fulfilling your goals and find people in your life. That you can share your life experiences with and find people that will take an interest and liking to you. Be careful of some people because they could turn on you. You can pick people like this. They are usually troubled with their own insecurities and worries within themselves. Rely on yourself in this world. Be your own best friend enjoy being in your own company and like who you are. Love yourself always.

Don't let anyone make you unhappy or upset. You have the control and ability not to let any person do this to you. People are usually like this because they are hurting within themselves. They are experiencing tremendous pain in their own lives. Some people can direct their own pain towards you with nasty and cruel words. Don't let this become your problem. Instead know that this is not your problem. It is all their own stuff. You don't have to be like them.

Stay away from such destructive people and get on with achieving your own goals. Be around people who encourage you who are positive towards you. You have your own choices and your own rights. Stick to what you know is right and best for yourself. Don't let your fears take control of you. Have courage in safe ways. Be thoughtful of your intentions with people like your family and friends. Show compassion and understanding to these people even if they don't respond in these ways towards you. Protect yourself from any destructive behaviour from anyone by distancing yourself from people like this. It is not good for you to be treated badly by anyone. If you are finding this to be happening have very little contact with.

These types of people. Concentrate on yourself with your own ambitions. Be around people who uplift your spirits who encourage and guide you in what you do. Stick with these precious special valuable important people. They are worth so very much and they always will. Look for the positives and good in people. Who you know and who you meet. Be an outgoing friendly kind person.

If you find someone in your family is mistreating you. Learn to block out their inappropriate behaviour you feel they are trying to put onto you. No person has the right to mistreat you. Just because they are experiencing pain in their own life. You can't change people like this. All you can do is change yourself with how you choose to react to them. When we are children we need our parents for guidance and security. When we become young adults it is time for us to move out of home. To start to find our own way in the world. Being capable.

As you get older you might feel at times that you are becoming distant from your family. This is because you are changing and they are also. You have now made solid friendships with people you call your best friends. You feel like you are independent and strong enough to live your own life away from your family. You still have contact with them but not as much as before because you are busy working studying going along to your interests. Having great times with your friends. This will all continue for the rest of your life.

As you get older you will change and so will your family. This doesn't mean their love will change towards you. You will always be in their hearts even when you aren't with them. Show respect to your family. If you find friction starting to build up have space from them for a while and that will mend your broken heart. Remember to forgive and love your family for any pain they might have caused you. Your family will always be there so try and learn how to get on with them. In ways that suit you the most. Try not to react to any unfair behaviour you feel they are putting you through. Be happy well balanced in control peaceful contented joyful relaxed at all times.

There is someone out there for all of us. It takes time to meet the right person. When you are able to be happy and content with what you are doing and you feel good about being the person you are. People who you meet will be attracted to these positive qualities you have. One day when you are not even expecting to meet anyone. You will meet that special person who you will not have any regrets about. From then on you will build the bases of a very strong relationship with trust compassion acceptance joy peace happiness.

It will last your whole lifetime. With anything in life it takes hard work trust understanding tolerance gratitude and good times. Whatever you want to see happen to yourself will happen. All in the right and best time. Don't take anything for granted. Be happy with what you have got in your life. Make positive steps into improving and bettering your opportunities gradually. Start off small and work your way up into success that you will be happy with. Make every year an achievable and exciting one. Try not to be sad and unhappy.

Be the opposite always be happy. Organize things that you will enjoy and you will look forward to doing. Your family and friends have and are moulding you into the person who you are. By there wonderful influences they have guided you with over the years. Appreciate your family and friends because without them you wouldn't be the person you are to this day. God has good opportunities install for you. God is a God of hope and love. God will continue to bless you in your life.

Without God love wouldn't exist and there wouldn't be good things in life. Never ever lose hope because God has got a lot of exciting opportunities ahead of you in your future. Take pride in who you are. Look after yourself in healthy ways. Don't take on other peoples negativity you feel might be directed towards you. People like this are suffering within themselves with their own issues in their own lives. Choose your friends very wisely. Be around people who are trying to make something of their lives. Who are trying to achieve their goals. Don't spend most of your time with people who haven't.

Got the same drive as you to succeed by getting ahead in their lives. It won't benefit you in any way in the long run. Be around people who are positive and who are making the most of their lives. This will help you to grow to learn to succeed in your own life. In positive and productive ways. Make the time to reflect over the good memories of your past. Think back and remember all the positive things you have achieved. Look at the strong friendships you have made with the people who are your friends. They are your true friends now.

Look at the wonderful coping strategies you have. That helps you to handle the difficulties that arises with your family. Look at all you have got coming up for yourself in the near future. You have interesting fantastic amazing incredible opportunities that will help you to grow in stronger and better ways. This will help you to build on and attract a more helpful and useful character. Every difficulty you get through will add to your strength of character as a person. Get out and discover new and interesting things you can do.

Be determined and motivated to take those steps of adventuring into the world of new and exciting opportunities. That are there so start today on your adventure of finding some things you can do that will bring you happiness. You'll be amazed at your results and rewards. Find out what interests you the most with people of your favourite choice. Use your gifts and talents with these people. Make what you have always wanted to see happen for yourself to become your reality. You know what steps to take to achieve your goals.

You know how you can do this. Work at tapping into your strengths and use these strengths into helping yourself to achieve your goals ambitions aspirations dreams. It is good to practice to not place any kind of judgement on anyone you meet. It is important to accept people just the way they are. If someone hurts you it is important to forgive and love them. For your own cleansing and growth as a person. Don't go out of your way to be nasty to anyone who has hurt you. This isn't as easy as it sounds because our natural reaction.

When someone has hurt us is to say something that we think might hurt them. Sometimes we do need to stand our ground with people so they don't get the better of us so they don't walk over us. In some situations it is important to know how you can stand up for yourself in an appropriate calm affective mature assertive way. Take your time getting to know new people. Choose your partner wisely. Don't settle for second best. There's no need to rush into any relationship with anyone. It is better for you to wait to meet the right person.

Who will meet your needs completely who will treat you well. With respect kindness goodness love forgiveness compassion. Rather than having a relationship with someone who doesn't have these qualities. Save yourself for that special genuine sincere honest trustworthy person. Who will enter into your life when it is meant to happen. When you are not looking for it. Find constructive things you can do in your time. It takes your planning organizing skills to practice using your time well. Make a list of all of the things you would like to do. Think of how you can go about applying these.

Things into your days when you aren't working. Spend time during the week looking for a job. Line up interviews from your local and general new papers. We all like to feel like we have a purpose here on this Earth. The more you are out there and involved in work and at your interests. The happier and more satisfied you will become. These two things are both the most important things in life to make you happy. Also being satisfied with your own achievements.

Will help you to have more confidence and self esteem. If you really want to achieve anything that your heart desires you can. When you are able to have a clear direction of what you want to achieve. The next step is to discover how you are going to be able to go about succeeding with achieving your goal. If you really want to do something then you will do it. You will try all that it takes from yourself to reach your goal. Never ever give up trying to succeed. When you don't give up that's when you will see your astonishing.

Results of your own success. You have got the potential and ability to achieve absolutely anything you want. Believe this and know this and just do it. Don't force anything that you want to see happen for yourself. Let what you want to see happen to yourself happen naturally. When it is meant to happen to you. Be happy and content in your own company. Make being on your own an interesting adventure of doing what you like and enjoy doing. Each day try and add something new to that day. That you haven't done before.

It could be something big or small. Just as long as it is something that has interested you and you have enjoyed doing. If someone puts you down know that they are being that way because they have got their own troubles and worries. That they are having to deal with. If this is happening continuously with a particular person in your life. You need to work out for your own well being and survival. What you can do as a mature adult so this won't affect you so much by interfering in your own life. Naturally at first this will affect you. Work it out.

If anyone is critical towards you. It is what you tell yourself that will help you to cope with such criticism. Knowing that you know that you are a good person who means well. Who is kind loving good to people around you. With people like your friends and people you come in contact with throughout your days. Is really all that is important and all that matters. It doesn't matter at all what other people think of you. It only matters what you believe to be true about yourself. Learn to switch off from people who criticize you.

Who try to bring you down in a nasty way. People get jealous bored frustrated within themselves. They get lonely and then there are other emotions. Tied into that we all go through every day. The most important thing that matters the most is how you yourself feel about being you. Spend time working out all of the positive things you have got going for yourself. Remind yourself about these strengths you have every day. To help you to get through your difficulties. To help you to survive in your life. In time you will continue to get stronger.

And wiser you will grow and mature more and more every day of your life. Don't let anyone drag you down. You know you don't deserve this. You are worth so much more than this. Like the person you are. Be comfortable and happy being the person you are. Learn ways of coping with difficult people in your life. Look at the difficult people in your life in a positive way. It is strengthening you into a more capable and courageous person. If you can handle these difficult people then you can do absolutely anything and everything.

You can handle any other person that you sense friction and tension with. Make a wonderful life for yourself. Full of enjoyment and great times. Let go of the painful memories of your past. Deal with these memories by knowing that the past is gone. It will never return in reality. The bad experiences you went through are gone. Focus more on the good memories you have from your past and what you have got to look forward to in your future. This will make you feel better.

By helping you to get involved with work study interests of your choice. By giving you strength hope confidence maturity wisdom fulfillment. With anything you do in life there will be a positive and negative side to it. There are positives and negatives with how you feel with your family. When you work in a job there are good things and not so good things about the job you are in. You might find that you clash with someone you work with. That could make it difficult.

For you to be there in that job. There are strategies you can take to help you to handle people you feel you clash with. It takes trial error tolerance. God knows everything about you.

God adores you Greatly. Turn to God even in the toughest times. You will get comfort from God through your most challenging times. God is there to listen and to answer your prayers. God is full of kindness goodness love compassion sympathy empathy forgiveness. When you feel like you are suffering Greatly turn to The Lord Jesus Christ Almighty. God has put you on this Earth for a reason and purpose. Without God no one would be alive on this Earth. In life when people are jealous of you.

And envious of what you have got that they haven't got. They can do and say all kinds of cruel and hurtful things. This is apart of life. You need to remember that it isn't at all your problem if someone is nasty towards you. Know that that is their own problem and stay away from these kinds of people. People like this do exist. Some of them have a more nasty attitude because they are unhappy within themselves. We all feel insecure in our lives it is part of being a human being at certain times. You have the power and control.

To overcome any difficulty you are experiencing at this point in time of your life. Use your strength wisdom common sense. To tackle your difficulties head on. Make sense of what is driving you to feel unhappy in your life. Try and find out what will ease your hurt and suffering. You are experiencing by finding healthy comforts as a substitute. It is hope that helps us to continue living in our lives.

Hold onto the hope you have. That will see you through all you are going through in your life. We all suffer with difficulties every day of our lives. The difficulties we go through make us stronger wiser more determined resilient motivated capable. You will grow greater. Try not to think of the worst. Instead think of all of the things you have got to be grateful for in your life. And what you have got to gain out of the situations you go through.

When other people see you going ahead in your life. They can say all kinds of things to bring you down.

Not every person is like this. You will find that some people will praise you and encourage your success and zest. The people you find that are bringing you down. Are probably jealous of you because they can't do what you are doing. Remember this and don't take any notice of such people. Don't let these sorts of people affect you in the slightest. Know that you are a worthwhile person. You are just as important as they are. We all get knocked down by other people in this life. It is apart of the process of living as human beings. With this it helps when you like the person you are faults and flaws and all. When you learn that it doesn't really matter what other people.

Think of you there will be a select few people that will be your faithful true lifelong friends. Who will like you for who you are. Who won't judge you they will accept you just the way you are. They will also stick by you through the good and the bad. People who criticize you aren't worth knowing. God has a plan for you. Ask your Father God in Heaven to reveal to you your deepest wishes. In time your Father God in Heaven will unfold these desires and wishes to you.

When God decides it is right for you. Remember to forgive those people who hurt you. Also remember to say sorry to The Lord Jesus Christ Almighty about the sins you make. Jesus Christ is your Saviour and Jesus Christ will decide when he wants you to be with him if you believe in Jesus Christ. We don't know when our time will be up. We will either have a short or a long life here on this Earth. We can only hope that we will be alive until we are of a ripe old age. God knows.

Now's the time to start planning by doing what you have always wanted to do the most. Having a fulfilling life is what makes us interesting. With more communication on different topics. It makes us more attractive when we are meeting people. It also gives us growth of character. It gives us confidence and it helps us to be happy. People you meet will notice these qualities you have. Some people will like how you are and will want to stay in contact with you because of the positive qualities you have. Your true friends will stay.

That they were drawn to from you. Originally with your first encounter when you met them. It works the other way also you will be drawn to the positive qualities of others that you admire the most. You will meet people as you get older. They will become your friends. Some people will be your friends for a number of years. Then you will both decide that it is time to branch out and move on. You will make new friendships with other people. Who you will start to form new friendships to replace your old friends. That you are no longer in contact with. Some of your other friends that you have known for years will stick around if they are meant to if you want.

Them to and like wise some of your friends will feel threatened by your success and they won't want to know you. Some of your other friends will feel grateful and privileged they know you. They will encourage your success. They will want to be around you because they feel you are inspiring them in their lives. With their own success that you are helping them to discover about themselves. Take a moment to look at the progress you have made throughout your life.

You have gone from making small steps into making bigger steps now. Look at yourself now where you are at. Ask yourself this question. Are you happy about where you are at in your life now with what you are doing. Knowing what you want to do and where you are headed with a clear direction. Are the first steps of making progress into a wonderful life for yourself. God works in mysterious ways. God sees the good deeds you do with your intentions of your heart. God knows everything about you. God has been watching.

Over you since the day you were brought into this world as a young baby. God will continue to watch over you and God will answer your prayers. For the rest of your life here on this Earth. Forgive and love your enemies. Remember to say sorry to The Lord Jesus Christ Almighty for all of the sins you make. Ask your Lord God to forgive you. God will always love you no matter what just as long as you Honour Worship Glorify God every day of your life. God is love.

If you believe in The Lord Jesus Christ Almighty then you. Will join your Lord God in The Kingdom of Heaven for all of Eternity. When God decides it is the right and best time for you to be in Heaven with your Loving Father Lord God. And your past dearly loved ones that made it to Heaven with God. Remember what your deepest desires are. Think about how you are going to go about making these desires become your reality. When you want to do anything that is the first. Step of making your dreams to come true. You have got what it takes to achieve your desires. Every day of your life that you live is making.

You a stronger and more capable person. For bigger and greater things to come in your future. When you find out what you are good at and suited to for work. It will get a lot easier for you to work on your skills with work experience and study. Then eventually finding the right contacts to go for job interviews. Then working in a job where you are meant to be at. That you will enjoy attending. The more interviews you go to the more experience you are gaining.

Then the more attractive you will be to an employer for employment. Think of the goals you have in place to achieve in the next 6 months. Work out how you are going to go about succeeding your goals. Making small steps each day will add to your progress in the long run of achieving in the end. There are so many things for all of us to work on in life. That's what makes our lives worthwhile and worth living. When you can prove to yourself that you are able to.

Follow through with achieving your goals. You will gain in confidence strength wisdom and your well being will be better. Any challenge you get through gives you strength of character and it adds to your optimistic view of your life. Enjoy the time you have on your own. Organize things you can do that will inspire and will interest you. Each day do and try something different to add to your list of activities. There are so many things to do in life. When you have an idea of what you would like to do. That's the first step of entering.

Your discovering of exciting and wonderful times that are yet to come in your life. God knows every thought desire dream you have. God loves you and God wants you to be happy. When you can forgive people who hurt you. You are cleansed for the sins you have made and you are also forgiven. God is the creator of this whole world. God will protect you and God will love you for the rest of your life here on this Earth. Always and Forever Honour Worship Glorify your Loving Father God. We all have Angels with us protecting us. Be your own best friend in your life. The only person you can rely on is yourself. People have their own lives to live. Value and appreciate.

The times you have with your friends. Show them you care about them by listening to them by offering your support. When you think it is best. Knowing who you can turn to when you are going through something difficult. When you feel lonely will help you along the way in your life. The more things you get involved in then that will give you more opportunities to meet more people by making more friends. Stand on your own two feet in your life. If your family.

Doesn't provide you with the support and care you need. Find this support and care elsewhere in people like your friends. Having faith in God by knowing that you are going to be okay will help you enormously. There are caring and loving people out there. It just takes time and being in the right place at the right time to meet these people. There will always be hope for you when you can seek it. What's the point of being around people who don't offer you the support and care you are looking for. God will guide you to people.

Try and mend the broken ties you have with either someone in your family. Or it could be with a friend that you fell out with recently. That you think you would like to patch things up with them. As life is short it is important to realise that people like your family and your close friends. Are the ones that will see you through in your life. No matter what altercations you have had with them in the past. What you project towards people like your kindness love goodness care.

Support understanding consideration thoughtfulness. This is exactly what you will receive back in return. When you show enthusiasm and encouragement towards people. By asking them questions about themselves with what they do in their lives. People love this and then they will do the same in return. Then both of you will be happy. This is what friendship is all about. Listening to another person and offering your support. Then it will work the other way as well. People will show you more respect and consideration when you apply these attributes. People will look up to you in an honourable and an significant way. Every time what you give out you will get back.

Be prepared for the challenging times that will be ahead of you. Have coping strategies in place to help you to handle these challenging times. Remember all of the efforts you put into your friendships. With handling your family especially in the difficult times. In the good times at work study at your interests. All of these things will pay off extremely well in your own favour. You will experience feelings of contentment happiness fulfillment. You will be proud of your achievements when you have completed them all. Stay positive.

You will grow in confidence you will gain knowledge and wisdom. Take the time to think about everything you should be grateful thankful appreciative for from time to time. This will help you to be satisfied and content within yourself. Being content and comfortable with who you are will help you in all aspects of your life. When you like who you are on the outside and on the inside especially. This will help you to go along way in your life. Following through with all of.

Your commitments that you are doing at present. Will benefit you enormously in the long run. You will see the positive results within yourself and people like your family and your close friends. Will admire your ability courage motivation determination. As we get older our lives get better because we are gaining the experience of handling ourselves more maturely. We also gain more motivation. With our commitments bit by bit each and every day. Start off small with your goals and work your way up to the top. You can do it.

Work out the things that are making you unhappy in your life. Put your head together and work out solutions at the core of your unhappiness. You have all of the answers with all that you are going through in your life. You know yourself better than anyone else knows you. Start today by getting to the root of what is holding you back from making your breakthroughs. When you start on this path there will be absolutely nothing stopping you from succeeding by moving ahead in your life. You don't need a partner to be complete. You can be quite content and happy being single until someone.

Who is compatible who will meet your needs will come along. Have a full life by enjoying all that you do. When you can be happy within yourself and comfortable in your own company. You are then in a much better position to attract someone who is similar to you. You know the people who you can confide in. Stick with these people and keep your options to meet new people open until you develop strong friendships. With these few new people in your life. People will come

Life is an interesting adventure just how you want it to be life is how you make it. If you want a full life filled with what you like. You can make it happen this way. Start now into entering fabulous times that you will love and create times that you won't ever forget. That you will cherish and treasure forever and ever. There comes a time when we reach a point where we need to have contact with people we know. The things that drive us to connect with people is loneliness and boredom. Getting support from someone about something.

We are going through and the list goes on. These are some of the reasons why we feel we would like to have a partner. For the friendship and companionship of someone who we see is special and important to us. We all need to share our experiences with our family friends and our partner. That's what life is about. It takes time to adjust to being in your own company. When you can look into a career for yourself by organizing interviews to go to. Also to help you to get into a good career it is good to have some qualifications.

Behind you by studying in the field of your choice. The more you can apply yourself with work study and at your interests. The better you will feel about yourself. You will grow in confidence and self esteem. People who know you will respect you more also. Get to know yourself by finding out what inspires you. When you like who you are you are then in a better position. To know what your strengths are and you can use them in your every day life. Get in touch with what you have always wanted to do. Make a start by getting involved with.

These things you will gain so much when you start on this wonderful path. Something we are forever trying to handle is dealing with loneliness. Feeling lonely motivates us to have contact with our family and friends. It also motivates us to get involved with work study and our interests. None of us wants to always be on our own. We all want to have company and to fill in our time productively. Also we all want a partner to love for friendship and companionship.

We all need each other our family and our friends for company support care and advise. Going through bad times to reach the good times isn't such a bad thing. We grow through our pain into stronger and wiser people. We all have some form of comforts to help us to get through the hard times. We are faced with which gives us satisfaction and reassurance. How we cope with our daily struggles makes us the people we are. A person who can shrug off other peoples unfair criticisms is one to be admired. We all get affected.

By how other people treat us. We all want to be accepted and treated well but speaking in reality. The people in this world aren't all going to be like this towards you. In time you do learn how to handle people who criticize you and who put you down. When you can believe in your own strength and ability for your own survival. This will help you to know how to handle these sorts of people. In life there will always be two sides to everything you do. We all get hurt.

It is a part of life. People can say and do all kinds of hurtful things when they are either jealous. Or in a fret with something themselves in their lives or when someone else has upset them. You might just happen to be the very one that is a target for verbal putdown. In this situation you have to remember that you are an important and special person. It really doesn't matter what other people say about you to your face or behind your back. Don't let anyone bring you down. You are precious and valuable. Stick with those few people who are kind and loving to you most of the time. You won't go wrong this way. Try and find things to comfort you through the difficult.

Times you go through. There is a positive and negative side to everything you do. Don't spend time with people who put you down. These sorts of people are struggling with their own problems. They want to bring you down so they feel superior to you so they have one notch above you. Be around people who aren't like this. You will feel a lot better about yourself when you surround yourself with people. Who treat you with respect the majority of the time.

People who know you well will admire your strength of character. When you get involved with work study and your interests. It takes courage and determination to stick to your commitments because it won't always be easy at times. When you are involved with these commitments. There will be people who you will get on well with. There will be people who you won't get on well with. In every circle of people there will be one or two people who you will clash with.

Stay away from these people. You don't need to give yourself to these people. If you do you will only get hurt. Learn the right steps you need to take to protect yourself in these certain situations. Find out the things in your life that will bring you joy peace satisfaction happiness. It doesn't take a lot of effort to know what these things are. Life is too short to be bickering with each other in nasty ways. If someone you find is treating you badly try not to take it to heart.

Just shrug it off quickly in your stride. When you can learn to smile in situations like this. You will gain so much relief of your discomfort. Of the hurt that was intentionally directed at you. When you learn and discover the power and control you have within yourself. When you can learn to apply these powerful and rewarding skills. You will be amazed at your own results from your own efforts. Practice the ability of your skills of not letting peoples words get to you. When you find them to be hurtful. Let their words wash over you quickly. Don't focus on such negativity. You know their words aren't true. They are treating you this way because they don't think highly of themselves. They haven't got what you have. In other words they.

Are envious of you because you have a lot more to offer people in this world. God is on one side and you are on the other side and Jesus Christ is in the middle. The free gift of Eternal life is through your belief in your Father God. Anyone who calls on the Lord. For him to take over in your life. These people will be saved. There is a power that is within yourself. That can transform your life completely. Through the rebirth of your Most Highest Glorified Father God. The Lord Jesus Christ. Your Most Loving Glorious Father God. Is always there for you protecting you from evil. God is there.

God is pouring out God's Blessings and Rewards to you. With all of the real truthful most miraculous divine love honesty gratitude purity goodness strength inspiration courage gratefulness. That God is forever guiding you to along the way in your life. To teach you all of the most valuable and precious lessons. On the chosen journey and destination of your life. That God has especially created for you.

God loves you so much. God loves you that much. God planned for you to have life on this Earth. A good life. A full interesting and an enjoyable life. For you to accomplish and obtain a close. Meaningful Purposeful Rewarding Relationship. With your Beautiful Lord and Saviour The Lord Jesus Christ.

Forgive those people who don't make your life easy. Learn more and more every day. That you are a child of God perfectly and wonderfully made. To serve the right purposes.

Of the right attitudes that you have acquired from all of the lessons. That you have learnt from with the source and completion. Of God's Eternal Most Profound Magical Confidence Enlightenment. That God is opening you up to. To your soul into all of God's ways truths understandings realizations. When you reach out to God in complete honesty truthfulness gratefulness. God will assist every need concern desire that lies deep within your heart. When you wait for the right meaningful awakening revelations. That God has especially to reveal to you. In God's most surprising and amazing ways. Your faith you have in God will strengthen inspire uplift you. Give you peace rest.

Hope joy happiness to your soul. God will bless you with all of God's richest finest love goodness holiness wisdom truth Glory. God's most divine and astonishing love loyalty fulfillment enrichment endearment graciousness. God wants you to search discover to find God. In all ways in everything you do. Praise and Glorify God because God is the Master and Creator in everything. Everyone needs to draw their strength goodness understanding aspirations purity gratefulness thankfulness appreciation Gratitude in God. God is love.

When you accept and realize all of the most beautiful merciful amazing things that come from God. You will see how much your life is worth living in every delightful way. Such as God's wonderous surmountable forever lasting rewards. From your continual approval acceptance openheartedness love enthusiastic desire want and need your eagerness to know. The Lord Your God. More and more every day. Will help you to be uplifted inspired wise careful enlightened thorough. In all of your ways God will show teach guide help reveal.

To you everything God has got coming ahead for you in your future so perfectly. God has got your destiny over your life worked out completely all in the right and best ways. That suit and match your needs and desires perfectly. Allow God to reveal to you. Your purpose and mission that God has called for you to fill on this Earth. By asking God to discern to you the real truthful naturally gifted.

Strengths abilities talents that God has given you. To use affectively and effectively in the right suitable and best areas in your life. Some people will hurt you they will make fun of you and they will desert you. Out of their shear disbelief uneasiness and from their own distresses and difficulties that they are facing in their lives. Just like you are dealing with. Hold on strongly with all of your strength hope thankfulness and gratefulness. You have in your Most Divine Forever Loving Magnificent Miraculous Heavenly Father God. God will bless you and reward you immensely in your life. God loves you a lot.

Every day make two three changes for the better. That are much more helpful practical thoughtful encouraging wise careful loving. For yourself and in the way you acknowledge help and treat your fellow man. Remember when you feel that you are in need of help and support don't be afraid to ask for help. Treasure and be grateful to God for everything. God has done and for everything God is doing for you at this present time in your life. God loves and values you.

That much that Jesus paid the price of dying on the cross. To save your from your sins. By giving you the chance to spend all of Eternity in Heaven. With your Most Divine Sincere Dedicated Courageous Unconditionally Loving Father God. Every day explore different and new ways of spending your time. Try to discover helpful ways to enhance improve on build on your awareness of what your purpose is. The more contented well respected peaceful consistent confident resourceful. You will become within yourself. You will see how you.

You will change for the better. From all of your continual productive efforts. Rely on your inner strength hope peace joy happiness inspiration courage. That God has placed within you. To manage to be able and willing to cope. Well in every situation and circumstance that God is guiding. For you to enter and experience. If you are struggling with something in your life. Turn to a close friend and seek their support. You will see how much better you will feel. Life's good.

Anything you wish to acquire and achieve for yourself will come true. If you make the right steps to fulfill your dreams. Pray to God about your concerns and difficulties. By asking God to help you in all of the right and useful ways. For you to have a comfortable interesting healthy meaningful well balanced rewarding happy life. Every situation you have experienced by living it and learning from it. Every situation that you have yet to experience and learn from. God is as God has always been at the centre. At the most implicit part of you. God has promised to remain your Saviour Guider Comforter Deliver.

Especially when you feel unsure doubtful confused saddened disorientated hurt upset. Turn to your Father God by sharing with God. Your despairs uncertainties hopes desires and dreams. To be fulfilled in peaceful contented satisfying pleasing keen eager enlightening ways. Know that your Father God is always there for you. Whenever you are in need of help. Hold on strongly to your faith love hope you have in God. To help you to ride through up and over. Your most difficult and troublesome despairs. Life is good.

There is nothing too small or too great that God can't intervene with. Through God's unconditional love care value importance understanding acceptance God has of you. God will help you through God's ever present omniscient gracious empowering positive Gloriousness. With God's perfect peacefulness goodness magnificence. God blesses and rewards those of God's children righteously. Who follow God's ways who honour and believe in God.

Your Lord God Christ and Saviour. God knows you and understands you the best above all people. God has made you by creating you all for God's truths love insights laws revelations Glory. Put all of your trust hope love faith. In your Most righteous perfect Gracious Father God. God will protect you from danger and evil. Be careful and weary of some strangers. Not everyone is kind good loving honest genuine. Be careful aware alert cautious patient protective honest sincere confident considerate comfortable wholesome happy being you.

God has overcome the world. By sending Jesus Christ Almighty to die on the cross. By saving you from your sins. God has given you the gift of Eternal Life. In The Paradise of Heaven with God For all of Eternity. The more you turn to your Father God. In times of despair sadness sorrow fear reluctance. Your own self insecurities uncertainties doubts anxieties hurts upsets. You will see the work and power and the movement of God transforming you completely. From the inner most deepest and most beautiful place. Where God lives and dwells within you. God will remain with you forever on Earth and in Heaven.

God is the source of all love hope victory welcome support peace goodness amazement endorsement courage gratefulness. The closer and the more real and intuitive. Your faith love hope in God becomes. When you open up by expanding within your whole soul completely. You will notice see sense the real prominent loving and nurturing presence of God. Working moving living in your life.

To heal and remove all of your sadness anxieties worries despairs concerns frustrations grievances. The closer you will become to learning knowing understanding God's ways and laws. By applying and living to the plan. Characteristics correctness respectful goodness compassionate caring calm nourishing plentiful ways from God. You will thrive in every positive healthy happy way in your life.

God has got all of the answers and control over every person that exists on this Earth. God is the founder of all of the mysteries reasons purposes missions of all human life on this Earth. God has given all of us free will. To choose to follow and believe in God or not. The world as it always has been every persons life. Has its own time and purpose to serve on this Earth. Some people will like and enjoy being with you. Other people won't like and enjoy being with you.

It is okay to be disliked and despised by people. That will make you a stronger and a better person. When people mistreat you deeply. God will comfort you and love you. When people don't care about you. God will bless you and reward you. When people reject you. God will embrace you and accept you. Just the way you are faults and flaws and all. Your life as like every other persons life is in the complete loving caring restful supportive victorious hands. Of your Most courageous faithful divine prestigious forever Glorified Lord Saviour. The Lord Jesus Christ Almighty. There is a better place awaiting for those people who Believe in. Who Trust in and who Honour Your Lord God Almighty. For each person on this Earth everyone has been given challenges to learn from and to grow in strength and ability. For your continual insights progression joy your own workmanship.

By knowing completely by trusting understanding believing. That on the bigger picture. God is as God has always been carefully with you watching over you. Ever since you were a young born baby. If you ever feel afraid or unsure about anything in your life. Turn to God in prayer. For God will guide you to all of the right practical eventful and best places for you to be in your life. Be careful aware cautious of what information you reveal of yourself to people who you sense you can't trust. Choose your friends carefully and wisely.

Be aware that out of jealousy disrespect misconceptions from some people. These people treat you in these ways and morals. Because they feel threatened by you and jealous because you seem to have it all. Continuity efficiency you adjust to change quite easily. You are attractive smart intelligent confident at peace joyful happy. You have awareness knowledge you are in touch close in tune to God.

At every moment of every day of your life. Praise by giving thanks to your Heavenly Father God for everything God has done for you. Praise God for all that God is doing for you in your life now. Hallelujah Praise God your Father God Almighty. God will never ever let you down. Be careful of what and when and who you conceal. Your own personal plans your gifts ideas strengths abilities desires and your future further goals and ambitions and dreams with.

As not everyone is worthy and deserving of your time and attention. Don't have anything to do with people who you feel and sense you can't trust. Avoid and stay completely away from inconsiderate demoralizing disrespectful senseless people. Always remember that God is on your side. Helping you to create by making a wonderful divine significant spacious collectable life filled with all of the richest goodness. Purity wholesome trust honesty delightful delectable dedicated forgiveness and courage. That God is continually giving to you. In return through God's gifts blessings rewards favour of you. You are acknowledging your Father God in every way by Glorifying and Praising your Father God Almighty. For everyone of the difficulties that God has taken away from you. By replacing your sorrows despairs anguishes. With God's Amazing Love Grace Comfort Strength Patience Forgiveness Confidence Awareness Peace Courage Gratefulness Appreciation. Have the faith love hope trust that your Heavenly Righteous Father God. Will bring you up through all of your fears doubts sorrows despairs uncertainties insecurities. Your faith you have in your surmountable conquering positive empowering.

Lovable graceful answerable Saviour God Almighty. God has saved you from all danger and unhappiness. God has placed God's Complete Joy Peace Happiness Patience Goodness Intelligence. All of God's Promises that God holds for you. To experience in your life. That God is making known to you. As the days go by. Your Love Trust Hope Appreciation Gratefulness Inspiration Enthusiasm. For what God has and is doing for you at every moment at this point in time.

Is growing in strength maturity hope integrity wider and broader understandings views and ideas. As God Instigates you by leading you to the Perfect Goodness Fulfillment Enlightenment. In all of God's Miraculous Supernatural Profound Truths Messages Insights Navigations Realizations. Trust that your miraculous Lord God. Will place you in the right and practical job in the right and best time.

God will bring you a future loving faithful dedicated thankful appreciative grateful sincere genuine husband or wife and children. In your life all in God's Most Prominent and Surprising Timing. Remember to put your time and energy into firstly. Your faith love hope you have in your loving faithful Father God Almighty. Secondly your relationship with your special friend and your other existing friends. Thirdly your career by realizing if you want to get ahead in your future. With bigger plans you need to be ambitious reliable becoming a quick and intelligent thinker. You also need to be patient keen positive well presented enthusiastic contentious. You need to be willing to learn and to be of help and assistance to people.

God has got your life all worked out so perfectly. In all of the right and best ways. That match and suit your needs and desires so perfectly. There is a reason for everything that you question and wonder in your life. Maybe one of the reasons why you haven't as yet been able to find employment is because God has chosen you to reach out and search for God. You can spread all of God's good news and revelations down through this generation. There is Power and Healing through Acceptance Understanding Forgiveness. God is love.

When you Forgive Accept Understand people who hurt you. Who ridicule you and disapprove of you. Who don't show you any compassion and respect for you. Your heart and soul will be Healed Flourished Nourished Blessed Filled with God's Purity Holiness. God's Everlasting Love Dignity all of God's Wisdom Fairness Safety Faithfulness Contentment. God will place everyone of God's Highest Sovereign Qualities Gifts Strengths Powers within you. As you become more and more like your Worshipable Pure Righteous Redeemable Perfect Father God Almighty. God is very Powerful.

When you are able to love and forgive people who mistreat you unfairly. Then you will be loved and forgiven and blessed by God. Get and raise your total awareness and continuity. From your Miraculously Divine Outstanding Father God Almighty. God is always keeping you safe and well protected. In every situation and circumstance you will ever go through. God will comfort you.

Every time you feel worried troubled despondent. God will Enrich Inspire Strengthen you completely. God will give you

God's Goodness Honesty Gratefulness Courage Truthfulness Happiness. That will keep you feeling energized enthralled positive alive empowered always and forever and ever. On Earth and in The Paradise of Heaven For all of Eternity. You have been given an judgemental disapproving undermining disinterested unsatisfying critical mother. For you to learn more and more about God. God is always with you forever.

God is helping you to find your True Passions Strengths Gifts Abilities Potentials. Everything that has ever and will ever be known to you. Has come from your Heavenly Maker The Lord your God. Ask for God's guidance ask God to reveal to you. What God has for you to be serving and accomplishing as your real and perfect purpose in your life here on this Earth. Raise your awareness to your Higher and your Truest Most Radiant Peaceful Joyful Happy Alert Sufficient Comforting. Safest loving forgiving good all of your most prominently rich dedicated faith love hope you have within yourself and you.

Have in your Father God Almighty so strongly and powerfully. May you always strongly believe and know from the deepest part of your soul. That God has got all of the Forever Comfortable Fathomable Answers to all of your Queries and Notions of the Purpose of your life. You have nothing to be afraid of or fear because God has conquered and overcome all mankind. From all sin and evil. By sending God's son The Lord Jesus Christ Almighty to die on the cross.

To save you and every other person. Who has decided to Believe in Trust in Love Worship Follow to be Faithful. In all of God's Righteous Pure Thankful Redeemable Honourable Grateful Appreciative ways. God has saved you from your sins. By sending God's Son Jesus Christ Almighty to die for you. For you to have a close inspiring uplifting meaningful empowering awe enlightening insightful purposeful.

Relationship with your Desirable Loving Caring Supportive Lord your God. The Lord Jesus Christ Almighty. God will never ever forsake you. God has all of God's love to give you for All of Eternity Forever and Ever. On Earth and in The Paradise of Heaven Forever to Come Forevermore. Sometimes God won't allow an opportunity such as job to work out. For bigger better practical more suitable opportunities. That God has got coming ahead for you. To Excite Enthral Exalt Uplift you. For God to bless and reward you. By filling you Completely with God's Pure Holiness Love Integrity Compassion Endearment Strength Courage Forgiveness Gratefulness Joy Peace.

God has dealt each of us trials and challenges to overcome. With Help Strength Guidance Goodness Appreciation Intuition Sincerity Complete Wholesome Peaceful Ways of God's Everlasting Love. That God is showing you every day in all of God's New Forever Changing Insightful Uplifting Joyful Glorious Optimistic Strengthening Adventurous Ways. Those people who have chosen to dedicate their lives. To their Most Superb Divine Amazing Beautiful Incredible. Righteous Outstanding Magnificent Creator The Lord your Father God Almighty. God is love. God will be with you Forever and Ever.

You will be Blessed Forever and Ever in The Land on this Earth and in The Paradise of Heaven. Where God will Transform you into a Completely Wholesome Pure Sanctified Peaceful Holy Blissful Perfect Spirit. Where you will live in Complete Safety. God is with you.

Comfortably Protecting you Harmoniously Peacefully Joyfully Happily in The Most Highest place of all. The Kingdom of Heaven with your Lord your God and your past dearly loved ones. God's love for you will never ever die. God will love you for all of Eternity. On Earth and in Heaven. Trust in your Heavenly Most Divine Father God. Your life is Forever and Always in

God's Hands. Every waking and sleeping minute and hour. God's love for you is so Pure Almighty Remarkable Significant Righteous Forever Lasting. On Earth and to all of the Most Amazing Realms of Heaven for all of Eternal Life. With your Maker and Creator. The Lord Jesus Christ Almighty. God will save you.

The Lord Jesus Christ Almighty. You will be together Forever with those you were Most Dearly Loved by. Who you Cherished and Admired in your Life the Most. If you want a healthy prosperous long fit energetic strong fruitful life. You always need to be aware cautious careful willing able. To put in More effort awareness consistency. In the areas of your life. Starting with putting a complete end to all negative self destructive demoralizing people and habits. Only allow positive and empowering people in your life.

The only Perfect Being you can always rely on so Passionately and Confidently is your Most Amazing Empowering. Soul Provider your Father God Almighty. God knows you so well. God made you just the way you are. As you are in touch and you are connecting closer more aware of as you are trusting your Lord God Almighty more and more every day. God is Blessing you in such Supernatural and Majestic Ways because you Believe in Love Worship Honour Appreciate Glorify God for everything. That God has done and is doing for you now. By making you into an Honest Open Trusting Serious Faithful Loyal Dedicated Healthy Respectful Person. God won't forsake you.

Only your Lord and Saviour The Lord your God knows you well completely. God is the first to understand you to protect you to help you to bless you to teach you. To learn from your mistakes and to apply your new learnt lessons appropriately and productively in the right areas of your life. Everything happens in God's Perfect and Amazing Timing. All of the Predestined

Gifts and Rewards you shall receive. In God's Most Glorious and Majestic Timing. God is good.

Will be Greatly Appreciated and brought forward through the Nations of People in Different Countries all around the World. Your Gifts Abilities Strengths Talents will be used Greatly with all Appreciation and Thanks. With much Value Gratitude Genuine Consideration Compliments. To every person who you will meet.

You are living to the plan of your life. That God has created for you. Everything has its own time place purpose. The more you expand your Inner Most Sanctified Tranquil Self. Through looking after yourself. Firstly Caring about Everything and Everyone that is in your life. That God has Kindly and Graciously Bless you and Rewarded you with. You will be amazed at all of the Most Truest Divine Perfect Majestically Honourable Righteous Things. That God will do for you in return. Be Happy at Ease Glad Grateful Fulfilled Contented Optimistic Useful Aware. Of making all of the right decisions.

That will benefit you and will suit you. In every Benefiting and Practical Way. Learn to really Love Cherish Treasure Acknowledge. Every Good and Glorious Thing that God has Kindly given to you. Your faith love hope you have in your Most Almighty Glorified Lord and Saviour. Has saved you from all of your sins. God has placed the Holy Spirit within you. For you to have the Strength Courage Unconditional Love Peace Safety Protection Gratitude Direction Discipline. Complete Joy Forgiveness Happiness. For a great life.

To last within you in every new unique and different way. At every moment On Earth and In The Kingdom of Heaven For all of Eternity Forever to Come. With your Most Beautiful and Amazing Father God Almighty. God is revealing to you each and every day. The right real true purpose of your existence.

Of what why when how the meaning of your life. Why you are here on this Earth. With what God has called for you to do. To achieve where when how you are meant to be serving your time. At the right places in the most useful practical rewarding ways. God knows what is best for you in your life always.

Shall The Lord your God fill every need and yearning you long to see happen for yourself. May God keep you closely and securely in God's Presence. Whenever you go and in everything you do. Now and Forevermore. There is more to yourself in this World. God is in Heaven with every person who lived on this Earth in the past. Who believed and knew God. In every Uplifting Compassionate Inspiring Loving Forgiving Appreciative Grateful Amazing Way. God is good.

God especially Protects Reigns Down On Blesses Rewards God's Perfect Beauty. To those who Honour Respect who are Grateful and Thankful of all of what God has done for you. By God helping you to learn all of the Right Useful Helpful Productive Resourceful Ways of Living your Life. In an Intelligent Organized Safe Thoughtful Successful way. Through the Insightful Empowering Enlightening . Of the Awakening of your Spirit of being Open Trusting Enthusiastic.

In Trusting God Completely. With a Strong and Optimistic Faith Love Hope in God. You are being led by the Omniscient Greatness Powerful. From your Saviour your Lord God Almighty. God knows what your needs and desires are within you. God has given you everything that is within you in your life. Through to your character traits. How you choose all of your qualities self attributes patience tolerance. The inner peace compassion forgiveness exuberance.

All that you have chosen to believe consider achieve create make happen. In God's Perfect and Amazing Timing. Everything that is meant to happen for you will work out. In the Right and

Perfect Plan of your life. That God has especially made for you. The people who mean something to you. Will Stand Firmly Strongly with your Enriching Joyful Insightful Empowering Loving Lord God who will never ever Fail you. Your faith love hope you have in your Lord God everything God is Teaching you and Showing you. God is there.

Is helping you to Shine from Deeply within your Soul. To help you to reach that Blissful Harmonious Relaxed Restful Stress Free Beautiful Glorious Place. That is The Paradise of Heaven with God where Everyone with God and Everything will be made Perfect. In God's Image. There will be no more pain no more suffering no more heartache no more sadness no more sickness no more hurt no more sorrow no more despair no more depression no more grief.

Everyone in Heaven and everything with God will live Perfectly Happily ever after always and forever and ever in The Paradise of Heaven For all of Eternity. Open yourself to the purpose and fulfillment of your life. That God is calling for you to enter to do to become. God will reveal to you in God's Perfect and Majestic Timing. What God has for you to do. Become aware of and look out for by Searching for the Signs Wonders Revelations Meanings. Of what why how you can go about finding out what your real and true. Gifts Strengths Talents Abilities are. Start by making the right steps into obtaining fulfilling making each of your Gifts and Talents become.

Your reality you are always at every moment in the Unconditionally Loving Purely Safe Genuine Comforting Sincere Arms. In the Complete Care and Guidance of your Most Magnificent and Glorified Father your Lord God. Your faith love hope and your trust you have in your Most Divine Holy Perfect Righteous Lord God Almighty. Is in the inner most essential core of every area of your life. When your faith love hope and trust you have. In God grows Stronger and Stronger. In More and More Loving Surreal Pure Divine in Open Minded Ways. You will feel and see how God will take away.

Your Uncertainties Sorrows Depression Doubts Fears Grievances. All through God's Eternal Love Goodness Safety Comfort Compassion Forgiveness Importance Reassurance. That God has got for you over your life. You will be quite surprised at how much. God really does love you and how God really cares about your needs and yearnings. When you are Open to God in Complete Trust and Honesty. You will be Quietly Pleasantly Surprised at the Inner Emotional Powers and the Changes. That God will Channel through every part of you. God will help you to Overcome all of your difficulties.

God will give you the Courage for you to Become Fearless. God has the Whole Picture. Of the making of your life All Worked Out Completely Perfectly. In all of the Right Practical Suitable Ways. That matches every one of your Desires and Ambitions Perfectly. God will always Protect you God will Bless you. God will lift up your Spirits. God will always Guide you to the Right Meaningful Insightful Purposeful Fulfilling Experiences. For you to dwell in Forever.

Where God has for you to be at the Right Timing of your Chosen Destiny. Created by your Most Faithful Regarded Genuine Beautiful Divinely Magnificent Father God. God will give you all of what you yearn for and God will give you everything you wish for from the deepest part of your soul. All in God's Most Precious Suitable Amazing Perfect Glorious Timing. God is always preparing by Organizing The Most Incredible Amazing and Outstanding Blessings. From all of your Good Helpful Kind Loving Fair Deeds and Works. That God has got to grant you. With God's Open and Forever Loving Arms. In all of the Best and Possible Ways. For God to reach you in every day. God made you the way you are. God has given you all that you have. With all of your efforts and hard work you are helping yourself with in the Inner Most Central and Close Guidance. From your Father God Almighty. Believe that God can help you to Change and to Recreate your World. You will then see how this will come true. The more you have faith hope love in God. When you believe.

Things will fall into place for you Perfectly. You create every one of your experiences qualities choices decisions characteristics. You are accountable completely of every step you make to becoming. What you have always dreamed to become. The more time you put in place for yourself. You will strengthen inwardly as you grow and mature. You will feel more and more comfortable contented joyful peaceful happy go lucky. You are learning every day how to improve.

Your Gifts Strengths Talents Abilities. Your attitude will see you through everything. You will ever experience. The Gratefulness Gratitude Patience Respect Goodness Forgiveness. You have for yourself and for your Faithful Loving Father God Almighty. And those people who you are closest to. Will always build you up in total Endearment Empowerment in Complete Joyful Enrichment Happiness Insightful. True and Fair Sincerity and Generosity.

God's Love for you is Infinitely the Most Unconditionally Ideal Powerfully Accepting Energizing Uplifting Courageous Nurturing Eternally Loving Forever. With God's Love you will ever come to Truly Understand and To Realize. That you will ever come to Relate to Perfectly. God is transforming you in all of God's Richest Faithful Enduring Insightful Forgiving Greatest. All of God's Purifying Ways every day. Your faith love hope you have in your Merciful and Glorious Lord your God. Is what has saved you from evil. God especially gives God's Complete and Total Goodness Honour.

Appreciation Respect Honesty Truth Wisdom Hope Strength Happiness. To those of God's Children. Who Love Honour Worship. Who are Grateful of what God has done and of what God is doing now in their lives. Praise and Thank your Heavenly Father as God knows what is best for you. God will Bless you and Reward you Abundantly. The More you are Open Willing and Able. To Work on and to Build a Strong Eternal Healthy Enriching Powerful Everlasting.

Relationship with your Lord God Almighty. Keep your faith love hope in your Magnificent Father God. God will be with you to bless you and reward you Forever and Ever. On Earth and in Heaven. God loves you more than you can ever imagine. God has got the power to Perform Supernatural Miracles on you at any given moment. Don't fret or become impatient with anything in your life ever. God is love.

Everything that God has to grant you. Is all in the Perfect and Most Outstanding Timing of your Life. That your Most Gracious and Courageous Father God Almighty. Has made for you to happen to you. In the Right Time of your Life. God has got your life worked out Perfectly. To suit and match every one of your qualities strengths ambitions characteristics. Start by initiating by looking into the things. Such as a career and interests that you know you will be able.

To achieve in and that you know you will be good at. Your eyes are for searching for your passions and making them all come true. Make a success of your life. In all of the ways that you know are good and best for you. To match the taste and likings. Of your credibility and your interests. You are responsible and in charge of your own life. No one has got any kind of power or control over you in your life. Accept God yourself your Husband or Wife your true and your close friends. God is your Protector Provider Guider Worshipper Saviour Deliverer Redeemer Life

Line your Greatest and Only Hope you have got. That will ever exist on this Earth. From the beginning until the end of your time on this Earth and in Heaven For all of Eternity. God is Awesome.

Always hold on firmly to your faith you have in God. For your faith you have in God will take you to amazing places in your life. Don't be afraid or fear anything ever. Any person who is intolerant angry abusive. Who has got rude behaviour towards you. Won't be blessed and rewarded at all. When your focus faith strength trust hope. You have in your Most Delightful Divine Faithful Magnificent Unconditionally Loving Father God is always open strong hopeful.

You will see how God is always on your side. Through God's Holy Restful Peaceful Trusting Hopeful Faithful Joyful Magnificent Thoughtful Special Knowledge. Of God's Most Amazing Grace Mercy Honour. That God has given to each of God's Fellow Christian Believers. When you feel afraid unsure concerned doubtful. Pray to God about your insecurities. God has got all of the Perfect Answers for everything you have ever wondered wanted experienced.

God will always be there for you. To keep you safe to protect you from danger as God has always Promised. God will save you from all of your sins. Through the power of The Holy Spirit. That God has especially placed within your Whole Soul. Live your life as Jesus did. God encourages you not to allow yourself to get into arguments with any person. Who for no reason starts abusing you or harassing you.

As soon as a person for no apparent reason starts ridiculing you or blaspheming your faith you have in your Divine Sacred Holy Father God. Do what Jesus did when Jesus came to Earth Jesus turned a blind eye completely. Turn your back on people like this. Keep on walking swiftly and confidently. With your head held up high. Remember it takes two people to have an argument but the one person who God will truly favour more is the person who kept on walking. Who turned their back and who has chosen to be a peacemaker. By allowing the Spectacular and Magnificent Work of God. To flow through you in complete Unison. God has got all of the Control and Power over Everyone and Everything in this World.

God has every Blessing and Reward that God will give to you. When the time is right and best. There are valid reasons why you are having to wait patiently for things to happen. Use your time on building a stronger open minded insightful truthful honest acceptance understanding courageous. Your faith love hope in your Most Sincerely Honourable Almighty Lord God. For God has got all of the answers to all of your questions and the things you wonder about.

All you need to do is to ask God by praying to him. By asking God to reveal to you the things that you would like to know. God loves to hear your prayers. As people like yourself who are true and dedicated Christians. Will be the people that God will go to firstly to answer your prayers. In God's Perfect and Amazing Time. God will especially hand down unto you. Because of your purity love faith hope you have in your Father God your honesty compassion patience forgiveness efforts kindness goodness. That you have from God.

By allowing God to enter into your life. Seeing how instantly God's Powerful Insights Gentleness Loveliness Softness Inspirations and Miracles are placed within you completely. Kindly from your Significant Father God. God is guiding you in all of God's Wonderous Ways. To change you by making you just like God. In the same Most Beautiful and Significant Ways that God is. When you choose to live.

In God's Ways and not the worlds ways. God will Bless you and Reward you Forever. On Earth and in Heaven For all of Eternity. Your well being and your Spirit. Your mental and physical health will all work well according to how Close Aware Open Trusting Peaceful Rested Loving Caring. To those people you are closest to. How much you Believe in your Heavenly Saviour God Almighty. God can help you by giving you the knowledge understanding empowerment. For you to deal with and cope with efficiently in every situation you are destined to enter in your life. Remember to stop to think to plan to work out the pro's and con's. Then take your time to make your.

Decisions whole heartedly. Ask the right people such as your true friends for advice when you need to. If your Mother and Father shall abandon you. God will never forsake you. God will comfort you in times of uncertainty and despair. God will fulfill every need hope despair yearning dream. You could ever wish for in all of the right and best ways. That God knows is Perfect for you. God will change your world so Righteously and Peacefully. The more you choose.

To Place your Hand in God's Hand. By Trusting God with all of your Heart Mind Spirit Soul. By allowing God's Spirit to dwell in you Eternally Forevermore. God especially looks out for and Blesses and Rewards those of God's Children. Who are True Genuine Honest Real Dedicated Sincere Trustworthy in every way in their lives. People who live their lives Humanely Wisely Peacefully Respectfully. Who have a Strong and Firm Open Reflective Understanding Meaningful.

Relationship with The Lord Jesus Christ Almighty. Will be the people who will win in the end in every area in their lives. God knows every persons heart and intentions. When you give out Compassion Sympathy Empathy Positivity Kindness Goodness Love Forgiveness to people. You will see how these Blessings will come back to you in return. Pray that God will protect you by giving you everything you need. For you to have a Joyous Full Peaceful Happy Courageous Enlightening Life. Always follow your Passions. God will heal you.

Follow the things that you know you are best at. Skilled at and Gifted in. Create an Exciting Inspiring Fulfilling Meaningful Sustaining Adventurous Life for yourself. Always give your Kindness Goodness Generosity to everyone. God always sees this in return. God will Bless you and Reward you with a Healthy Secure Happy Well Balanced Well Educated Well Adapted Future. That you Most Truly deserve. God's Love for you is the Most Purist Sensual Worthy Motivated Inspiring Unconditional Loving. That you will ever receive. That you will ever come to truly understand and experience. The Relationship you have with your Almighty Faithful Father God.

Is one of the Most Important and Crucial Relationships you will ever have. As we are not perfect. It is only human to misunderstand where some peoples views and ideas are coming from because we are all different. There are few people who will accept you and understand you completely on a similar level. As God's Blessing to you God has especially given to you. The Privilege and Honour of a very Special Open Loving Well Balanced Equal Respectful Genuine Sincere Friendship you share with your Heavenly Loving Father God.

And your Special Closest True Friends. That will last Forever and Ever on Earth and in The Kingdom of Heaven For all of Eternity Forever to Come Forevermore. God will decide when you have outlived your life. You are always at every waking and sleeping moment. In the Precious and Amazing Hands of your Most Divine Supreme.

Magnificent Lord and Saviour God Almighty. Your Heavenly Father God has sent Jesus Christ Almighty to this Earth to save us from our sins by dying on the cross. So we could have Eternal Life with God in Heaven Forever and Ever. Those people who seek to know by reaching out to God in prayer. For Thanksgiving Worship Insights.

Appreciation Understanding Compassion Goodness Kindness Forgiveness. Who Spread the Honest Sincere Truths Richness of God's Great Honour Wisdom Glory. Will be those Chosen People of God. Who will Live Happily Ever After on Earth and in The Paradise of Heaven For all of Eternity. The One and Forever Important Remaining Fact in this Life. Is your Respect Love Kindness Goodness Trustworthy Worthiness Compassion Understanding Honour Realizations. That you share with your Righteous and Merciful Father God Almighty. Nothing can ever break you. The More Open Minded Stronger Aware Willing you become by working on reaching out. To your Heavenly Lord and Saviour God Almighty. In Prayer for you to become More Peaceful Restful Calm Empowered Fearless Affective Independent Responsible Self Reliant Capable. The Happier More Delightful your Life you Live Each Day will become. Each of us have our own unique.

And Individual Right to be Ourselves to Accept that we are all Different. The Most Important Lesson you can ever learn in this Life. Is to always Surround yourself with people who are like minded to you. Who are on a Similar Wave Length as you are. As we are all different with our genetic make up. In terms of our Qualities Beliefs Strengths Expectations. In the Ways we have Chosen to Cope and to Survive in this Life. By those Caring Helpful Kind Hearted Good Willed Supportive Understanding Accepting people. Who have Stuck by you.

Through the Thick and the Thin in your Life. To help you to Overcome and Overlook your Challenges and Difficulties. In Productive Open Minded Sufficient Useful Calm Positive Peaceful Contented Wise Ways. Be Grateful Thankful Appreciative to God. For God has given you the Privilege of the

Gift of Life. Be Thankful and Praise your Almighty Father God. For allowing you the Opportunity to Spend all of Eternity in Heaven with God. God Loves you this much Forever.

God Blesses and Rewards those of God's Precious and Most Valued Children. Who acknowledge all of what God has done for you in your Life. God sent Jesus to this Earth to pay the price by sacrificing himself. By Dying on the Cross to Give you the Opportunity of Discovering God. By Knowing Seeing and Believing that God is Always Walking with you in your Life Every Step of the Way. God is with you.

Those people that have a committed open aware intuitive faith love hope in their Righteous and Most Loving Father God Almighty. Will be Cherished Blessed Protected Nurtured Strengthened Empowered by God. God will give God's Endless Most Miraculous Love Peace Goodness Stability Courage Wisdom Glory. Forever and Ever on Earth and in The Kingdom of Heaven For all of Eternity. You can never go wrong when you have a Strong Trusting Firm faith in your Heavenly Father God Almighty. God will always be there to catch you when you are falling. To make you Strong and Fearless just like him. Everything you have done said pursued agreed with responded with acted upon reacted to. Has been Created by God through learning.

Your Biggest Lessons through your Almighty Glorious Powerful God who is within you. From the Power of The Holy Spirit. God Dwells within your Whole Spirit. The Stronger and More Well Known your Understanding of your faith love hope in God Develops Grows Becomes. More and More Real Truthful Loving Forgiving Revealing Tolerating Accepting Compassionate Sacrificial. The Better you will Handle and Manage everything that is Destined for you to go through. That God has laid out for you on the Right.

And Perfect Path of your Life Created by your Most Honourable and Justified Heavenly Father God Almighty. The More you Depend on Building a Strong and Fulfilling Relationship with your Father God Almighty. You will see how God will help you in every way. By Fixing and Mending every difficulty. Where you have felt you have gone wrong. Through the Endless Love Grace Mercy Forgiveness Courage.

That God has to Inspire you with. Everywhere you go and in Everything you do. God will love you Forever and Ever. God will show you by Teaching you Closely how to Correct your Ways by Learning from your Mistakes Every Day. For you to have a Better More Pleasurable Rewarding Happier Life. With Internal Strength Integrity Hope Understanding Compassion Insights Inspiration Faith Trust Unconditional Love. A sense of Purpose that all comes from your Divine and Most Purely Significant Heavenly Father God Almighty.

God is making himself known to you. Through the Power of the Holy Spirit that has been placed deeply within your Whole Spirit. God is Revealing to you each and every day. The Real Truths Meaning Understanding. All of God's Great Insights Intuition Resolutions Wisdom. That will Change your Outlook and Perception. In every Peaceful Accepting Well Mannered Joyful Smart Articulate Empowering Glorious Way. God has given each of God's Children Challenging Problems so you can with all of your Strength and Will. Turn to your Father God Almighty. The Only Omniscient Soul Provider who knows everything about you so Sincerely Truthfully.

Passionately. Who made you just the way you are. Who has the Strongest Love Control Restoration Compassion Honesty Holiness Divinity Faithfulness Empowerment Enlightenment. That you are coming to see realize to apply in your own life. You are also discovering how there is Power in Forgiveness Trust

Strength Hope Faith Goodness Patience Courage. That all comes from your Heavenly Maker your Lord God Almighty. It is possible with God.

God has given all of God's Children trouble in some form or another. God has allowed for you to experience all of these emotions that Jesus went through. We have different opinions disappointments persecution from non Christians. We are all made to feel in some situations that this Life isn't fair. These feelings are completely normal and human. You need a Strong Loyal Genuine Committed Motivated faith in God. To work on every day for you to remain.

Risen by your Heavenly Father God Almighty within your Spirit. To allow the Continual Grace Mercy Goodness Kindness Eternal Love Gratefulness of God to work through you Sufficiently and Effectively. The Power of God is by far the Most Incredible Divine Amazing Significant Power. That will ever be with you Forever and Ever. Until the End of your time on this Earth and in The Paradise of Heaven. Where God will make you Perfect in God's Image. God will make you.

Perfect Joyful Pure Clean Righteous Peaceful Happy Positive in Heaven Forever and Ever. Don't be afraid of anyone or anything. God is always with you even in the Most Painful and Toughest of Times you go through. Show No Fear become Fearless Unafraid Loving Kind Hearted Grateful Thankful Appreciative Good Natured Compassionate. Especially to those people who are trying to help you with their best of intentions. Some people might not approve of you they may not understand you. They might see you in a very negative and displeasing way. There is no need for you to worry or let these people affect you in the slightest. Your Most Nurturing Loving Uplifting Empowering Enlightening Forever Blessed.

Sacramental Saviour God Almighty Loves you so much. God's Love for you is the Strongest Almightiest Perfect Pure Compassionate Everlasting Holy Righteous Love you will ever receive in this life. That you will ever experience in the next Life in Heaven when you come face to face with Jesus Christ Almighty. In the Real and Highest Realms. Your Father God will make Superb and Great Things happen to you in your Life. Your faith love hope you have in God is so Strong.

You are also Willing Open Able to be Close to In Touch Aware. Of the Word of God through the Power of the Holy Spirit that is within you. We all have difficulties in our lives that we are struggling to cope with. The difficulties that go through in your Life. Can feel Overwhelming Worrying Threatening to you. The Best Thing that you can do to start dealing with your difficulties one by one. Is to tackle.

Your Challenges head on by taking Small Steps that you know will help you to Cope better with your Struggles. When you start to feel Stronger and More Confident within yourself. You will be able to Overcome your difficulties. Keep on working on the difficulties that you know are holding you back in your Life. Start by Changing your Behaviours. You will then see yourself Entering a Brighter More Positive and Comfortable place in your Life. God Understands so.

Much how you feel with all of your Doubts Worries Concerns Insecurities Uncertainties Sadness Hurts Upsets. God wants you to hang in there through all of your difficulties and hardships. All of the Suffering you have gone through and you will ever go through. Will be Rewarded so Greatly from God in The Paradise of Heaven For all of Eternity. Where you won't be and there won't be anymore Suffering Worries Doubts Concerns Hardships for you to go through on this Earth anymore. You will be with God where you will be Perfect. You won't have anymore fears concerns difficulties to go through anymore. Suffering at times on this Earth is Worth it as your time will come when God decides it is the right time for you to be with God in The Kingdom of Heaven For all of Eternity. Thank God.

Thank your Lord God for those of your Wonderful Friends that God has Blessed and Rewarded you with. On the Path that God has Chosen for you. Your True Friends you were meant to meet were given to you from God. God has more people that you are Destined to meet in Places that God will lead you to go in your Future. When you feel all alone when you feel like your life has got no direction.

Trust in your Lord God Almighty. God has got Good Things Install God will make happen for you. Your family might not accept you and understand you but God Accepts Loves Understands you so much. God gave you your Personality with all of your Strengths Traits Gifts Talents Qualities Attributes Characteristics. May God help you by giving you God's Strength Love Peace Harmony Kindness Goodness Wisdom. All of God's Destined Blessings and Rewards which God.

Knows you Deserve and of God's Compassion Endless Love Special Knowledge Honour Glory. Everything that has happened to you in your life good and bad has meant to of happened to you. For Good Reasons that God knows of Completely. The Pain and Difficulties you have gone through in your past have happened to you so you could learn the right and appropriate ways to live your life. So you could discover by getting to know your Lord Jesus Christ Almighty.

Your faith love hope in God is what gives you the Most Strength Courage Goodness Kindness Hope Positivity Compassion Motivation Determination for you to Live Greatly by Surviving Well in this World. When you feel like there is no one around to help you for you to turn to. Know that God is Always and Forever with you. God will Comfort Bless Care Help Encourage Inspire Support you through everything. God will never ever abandon forsake or leave you. God is Walking with you through everything you Feel See Hear Believe Experience. Through all of your Worries Concerns Doubts Sorrows Difficulties you will ever go through. God is Always and Forever with you. God will Love you For all of Eternity on Earth and in The Kingdom of Heaven Forever to Come Forevermore. Forgive people who don't treat.

You well and who don't understand you. This is not your problem at all. This is their own lack of Sympathy and Understanding that they have within themselves. Ask your Lord God Almighty to give you More of a Purpose and More Direction in your Life. You might have been going through a difficult patch in the past year or 2 of not knowing how you can spend your time in Productive Beneficial Purposeful Motivated Ways. Ask your Lord God Almighty.

If God can help you by giving you a More Enriching Purposeful Meaningful Productive Beneficial Motivated Rewarding Life. God is with you through everything you go through. God Shall Heal you from all of the Pain and Hurt you experience in your Life. Through God's Most Powerful and Incredible Love Kindness Goodness Helpful Sincerity that God has got for you. Shall God Always Comfort Guide Love Protect Keep you Safe. Shall God continually Bless you Infinitely.

Through God's Strength Grace Hope Love Goodness Kindness Peace Joy Happiness. God will always Care Love Bless Reward Adore Cherish Treasure you in your Life Forever and Ever. On Earth and in Heaven For all of Eternity. God is very Understanding Patient Faithful Loving Forgiving Compassionate. God Accepts and Adores you just the way you are. When you feel that people don't treat you well.

Know that God really Loves Accepts Understands you. You are very Precious Important Special Valuable Worthy to God because God made you just the way you are. God wants you to be natural easy going patient for you to be yourself. In Contented Peaceful Out Going Relaxed Hard Working Ways. Have fun times when you are with your Friends. Your Beautiful Faithful Righteous Father God Almighty has so many more Blessings and Rewards that God will give to you. When God thinks it is the Best and Right Time. It is important to be Understanding Patient Accepting Tolerant Forgiving towards Everyone you know and to Everyone you meet. Be Kind Good Fun Loving Out Going. Be an Achiever and a Tryer make all of your. Dreams Come True. We are here on this Earth to Learn Grow to Fulfill all of our Dreams. God is in Heaven Always Loving Protecting Blessing Rewarding Inspiring Helping Keeping you Safe. By Leading you to Good and Supportive People. God is giving you all of God's Motivation Peace Joy Happiness which will remain within you. Every day God decides to give you to live your life on this Earth. Shall God always be close to you on Earth and in Heaven For all of Eternity.

You will feel good again after you go through any bad patch. Every day we are getting Stronger and we are Learning how to handle difficult people. As we get older we get better with knowing how to handle people by knowing what to expect. Be careful with what information you give to people because they could use it against you. Out of their Jealousy and out of their own frustrations in their lives.

Don't trust people completely when you first meet them. If you do you could set yourself up to get hurt. People can be deceiving. They might appear nice toward you but in time you will find out how they really are. God absolutely Loves you and Adores you Completely. You are important to God. We are all born into this world of sin. This has got to do with how we are all not perfect. As we get older we learn how to handle the challenges we are confronted with in more useful ways. You get use to the knock backs and disappointments in life.

Work on looking at what you go through in mature and sensible ways. To help you to get through these times. Every now and then you will come to a point where you will feel overwhelmed with what has been going on for you. This is part of being a human being. Just let yourself over ride these times. You will see how quickly these times will pass. Try and comfort yourself amongst the inner pain you are going through. Find out things what will sooth the hurt you are experiencing. Try and distract yourself from your struggles. Know that in life there will always be challenges to get through. Get to know what will help you to cope in your Life. All of us have to go down to be up again sometimes. This is the process of Life. Every day we are all like this. There will be good and bad in all that you do.

If you have survived all of your Life up until now. What is stopping you surviving the rest of your Life. Working on having a Positive Attitude in your Life. Learn to laugh at things that happen to you. Have the Strength to Overcome peoples unfair behaviour they are trying to inflict on you. This is a learnt skill. We are all trying to learn how to handle people when they do this to us. If you like yourself.

If you are Happy with being the person you are. What does it matter how people treat you. If it is negative and disempowering. Always be Strong and Determined in your Life. Learn to bring out the best in yourself with all that you do and learn to bring out the best in people. For some of us your Husband or Wife and Your Family and Friends will be the Ones who will see you through in your life always. Coming from a dysfunctional

Family is common. If you find your Family aren't offering you the Support and Care you are looking for.

Limit your contact with them. Be around your Husband or Wife and your Children and your Friends more by doing things that you will all enjoy doing together. These people won't judge you or criticize you. They will be completely the opposite because they Love and Care about you the most. They enjoy being in your company. They will stand by you through everything you experience because they know you the best. Find out ways to express the pain you experience.

It could be talking to a Friend writing down on paper the way you are feeling reading a book dancing to your favourite music exercising or listening to music and singing. We all need forms of outlets to release the pain and suffering we go through. Figure out what will help you to Overcome your Troubles. You will find out how much better you will feel about yourself when you do these things. These things will take you along way in your life. Remember to try and turn to these things when you are suffering or lonely. Nothing will ever be that bad that you won't be able to cope with. Go for it in your life. Strive to Always and Forever to be Happy and Content. You have got absolutely nothing to lose but everything to win in your life Forever.

Hold on to your faith love hope in God. God is there to help you even in your toughest times. God will see you through everything until the end of your time here on this Earth. God knows you are Precious Special Valuable Important Worthy like the rest of us. Forgive your enemies and all will go well for you in the Land. When you forgive people your Heart will be Cleansed with Pure Love. Pray a nice prayer for someone who has hurt you unfairly. Your faith love hope in God will see you through everything you will ever go through in your life.

God is the Creator of this Whole World. Without God none of us would be here on this Earth and there wouldn't be any Love and Beauty in this World. The hope we have for our Future is what sees us through in our lives. Having Good Friends is something we all need and appreciate and having a Partner who is compatible for our needs is important for our Survival in this Life. Think of the things you have got to be Grateful Thankful Appreciative for every day of your Life.

Try not to spend your time focusing on the negatives. You will feel better when you are in a positive frame of mind when you can be. Do what brings you satisfaction and happiness the most. Usually what we fear within ourselves seems a lot worse than what will actually happen to you in reality. When you can realize this this will help you to Overcome and Conquer your fears and this will help you to get on with things in your Life. Don't let anyone intimidate you ever. You know how not to let anyone do this to you. Always remain In Control.

And Calm with handling people even in the most Difficult Situations. You are a Worthy and a Deserving Person. Who has Qualities that will Benefit people in your Life. Stick with those people who make you feel Good about yourself and who bring you Complete Joy Peace Happiness. A person who can listen to another persons experiences is one to be admired. To put yourself in the other persons shoes with what they are going through is a learnt skill. People like it when they are listened to by other people. We all want to feel wanted and accepted by people. Some people won't like you but a lot of people.

Will like you and accept you. We are all attracted to particular qualities of each person. We know what you like and what you don't like about yourself and other people quite clearly. Get in touch with what you really want for yourself in your Life. When you know what you want then you can make the steps into making the desires happen for yourself. Have Goals to work towards always. Figure out what you are good at and use these Abilities more in your Life.

Have Supportive and Helpful Friends and be of Support to them. When you think about it Life is Short. Do all that you can to be Well Balanced Be At Peace Joyful Positive Happy. Work towards on having Good qualities and Good times in your Life. With the people you Love and Care about the Most. Any bad experience you to through something good will come out of it. People will do and say all kinds of hurtful things when they are jealous of your qualities as a person.

How you present yourself with what you wear and your hygiene is important every day. People appreciate people who go to an effort with their appearance. It is important to have a positive and healthy self image. It also helps to know your Reasons and Purposes why you are here on this Earth. Such as what Missions you are meant to be living in your Life here. When you discover and realize your Reasons. And Purposes here on this Earth. You will feel so good and alive within yourself. Make the most out of your situation in your life.

Work on having a strong shield in different ways every day. People don't mean to hurt you it's because they are going through their own hurt and pain in their own lives. Forgive and Love people when they hurt you. When you do this you will see how these people will come around in their own time. They might even grow to like you because you are Forgiving and Loving them. We all have a positive and negative side to ourselves. Try and get in touch with your positive side rather than focusing on your negative side so much. We all have control over what we tell ourselves with everything we do. You will find that when you are able to think positively more every day.

With what happens to you. You will feel better within yourself and you will be more Confident In Control of things and this will add to your Ability of Coping in your Life. With all of the Challenges that Life throws at you. You have to be Strong Willed to Survive in your Life. As there are so many Good Things to Always Learn in this World. Be Grateful for every Living Day of your Life. Work on being an Optimist rather than a Pessimist. You will know when you are ready for.

Anything you wish to do and achieve. In time we grow out of old habits the way we handle ourselves and also how we handle difficult people. We are Forever Learning with all that we go through in our Lives. Having Positivity and Hope is what keeps us Alive by Helping us to carry on. Treat people how you would like to be treated. Assert yourself appropriately with people when you think it is necessary.

Treat people Fairly. Don't let anyone walk over you. In confrontational ways with people you come across. Remember the people that like you who enjoy being in your company. We all have different qualities about ourselves and each of us have different ways of handling people. We learn from each other with our behaviour and our actions and how we communicate. A person who can ignore peoples hurtful words who can understand that they are.

Going through their own problems in their lives. Is a person to be acknowledged and praised. These people who can oversee and understand some other people when they get a bit short. These types of people will go along way in their lives. If you have understanding about other people this will help you to handle people by changing your behaviour and attitudes towards yourself and others. All of us have experienced some kind of trauma in our past. When you are able to learn through your trauma and pain. You will find how you will change as a person. It is healthy to experience change. By stepping out into the unknown in your life. Get in touch with your Gifts and your Strengths. We all have Individuals Strengths.

When you are able to discover them. They will take you right through. Your Entire Life until your time is up on this Earth. Work on your Strengths every day and apply them at Work your Friendships with your Husband or Wife with your Children at your Interests at Church with your Family. Learn to try and get on with people to a comfortable extent. When someone hurts you always Love and Forgive them. Then your Heart and Soul won't be bitter at all.

We all want to be accepted by other people. We all want other people to make us feel important. Lift yourself out of your hurt when you are feeling down. We are what we think of ourselves deep down. If you like yourself then other people will like you. Be Comfortable and Content being the person you are. Do Rewarding and Pleasurable Things for yourself. You will gain in satisfaction by doing.

These Rewarding and Pleasurable Things. It doesn't matter if a small majority of people don't like you. Look at the people that do like you. Try and Focus on the Positives in your Life. Always be Happy being the person you are. The More Work you put into yourself the more you will get out of Life. Look at the Beauty in the World that God has Created. It could be looking at a Flock of Birds flying above in the Sky. It could be seeing people who you think are attractive. It could be appreciating a kind gesture that someone has done for you.

These things in Life are what brings us Fulfillment and Happiness to our Hearts and Souls. The people we know like our Family and our Friends who mean a lot to us. Who make our Lives Worthwhile and Worth Living. Listening to music and singing and dancing to music brings a lot of Enjoyment Joy

Satisfaction Fulfillment to your Heart Mind Body Spirit Soul. Always be Thankful Grateful Appreciative for everything that is yours in your Life. Always be Kind Loving Good to everyone. Nobody can take away your happiness. Only if you give them the power for this. Teach yourself skills that will help you in all kinds of areas in your Life. Your Life is here to be enjoyed to build strong friendships with people to work at having caring relationships.

With your Family being Loved by your Husband or Wife. There is so much to get out of in your Life. When you know where you are headed with a clear direction. This will make it a lot easier to get you somewhere in your Life. The most important thing in Life is to Love. To give Love and to Feel Loved. The more you try in your Life in Positive Ways the more Benefits you will gain from yourself and from people who know you. You can handle anything that happens to you.

You will be able to cope every day for the rest of your Life. We all know what it is like to be down. It is a matter of practice to pull yourself out of these times. As we grow and practice doing this. We become More In Control More Capable Motivated and A More Likeable person. People want to be happy and people want to feel good within themselves. When you see someone's strength in something tell them. By Acknowledging them complimenting them.

Learn how to make people feel good about themselves. Remember what you give out you get back in return. Make things happen for yourself by using your Organizational Skills. When there is a will there is a way. If you want to go out and have a good time think of the people you would like to invite and go for it. It could just be one person. You can have just as a good time with one other person as well as a group of people. Your Life is how you are creating it and making it to be like. When you know how to spend your time.

You will start to feel like your Life has got Meaning you will also feel like you have got a Purpose in your Life. You will then discover just how much your Life is Worth Living. In Every Good Worthwhile Exciting Way. Be Patient when you are wanting to meet a Partner. Take your time with this there is no need to rush into it. There is someone out there for all of us. When you are able to wait you will unexpectedly meet the right person. At the right place at the right time wherever it maybe where and when it is meant to happen. Some of us find our True Love at an early stage in Life and other people find their True Love at a later stage in Life. God's Will.

God has planned your stay on this Earth. God has his reasons for you to be alive on this Earth. There is work to be done with your faith love hope in The Lord Jesus Christ Almighty. When you have faith love hope in God your Life will change for the Better in Miraculous Supernatural Inspiring Insightful Positive Enlightening Empowering Ways. God has given his Love to every Human Being on this Earth.

We have the Choice to Honour our Father God in The Kingdom of Heaven. When we have faith love hope in God by Living our Lives in Kind Good Loving Christian Ways. It will be up to God when God decides for you to join God in The Kingdom of Heaven For all of Eternity. Continue praying to your Father God Almighty. For anything that your heart desires for. Pray for people you know who are in need of God's help and healing in their Lives. God is always there.

Everything will work out in time. Be patient with things. When you are patient good things will come to you. Make every day of your Life one to look forward to. With work you enjoy going to. Friends who you enjoy socializing with. When you have interesting activities to go to. You will become more and more helpful wiser useful happier. You will also develop and mature in many Rewarding and Delightful Ways. To be Alive on this Earth is a Gift and Blessing from God.

Don't take anything for granted. Everyday of your Life is how you have made it and it is what you have put into your days. That is what you will get from it. Your attitude towards everything that happens to you. Is what sees you through it all. Reach out for the Light in your Life. The Light exists for all of us. It is a matter of finding the Light within yourself. When you discover this you will find your own inner strengths at work. With the Friendships you have with your Family and Friends. Reaching the Light provides you with a Shield. It helps you to know that it doesn't really matter. When someone seems abrupt or rude towards you. Because part of the Shield you have has understanding of other people. Look at the Challenges you go through in Positive Ways. Your Challenges are making you Stronger.

They are giving you Special Wisdom from God. You are also learning from your experiences. In any difficult situation these situations are giving you understanding acceptance courage knowledge strength forgiveness compassion. Train yourself to learn from your experiences. Don't be bitter towards anyone even if people aren't treating you well at all. Forgive and Love these people and show them an act of your kindness goodness love understanding. Life is too short to cause trouble. Always be a peace maker. God loves you.

Having someone else within your Presence takes away your concerns loneliness and it provides you with Support and Company. This brings us Satisfaction Purpose Joy Peace Happiness. We all need Company at Times throughout our Days. If it is at Work Studying Seeing Friends or Seeing Our Family. Doing these things is what helps us not to feel alone. It also helps us to feel like we have a Purpose. It helps us to feel like we are Helping People. We know who are in need of Help.

When you can listen to people and be of help by giving your words of advice. People will see you in a different light. They will automatically do the same for you in return. Don't compare yourself to anyone. We are all equal no matter what we do. We all have Different Qualities Abilities Attributes Gifts Talents to offer the World. Nobody is better than anyone. We are all Unique and Different. When you can think this way you will be Well Adjusted and an Well Balanced individual.

Work on using your Motivation and Abilities at Work. Where you Study. With your Friends and when you are with your Family. Always have Friends who treat you well. Let your Friends and your Family Husband or Wife and Children. Know how much they mean to you. Look at all of the things you have in your Life to be Grateful for such as your Friends. Your Family the House where you Live. Where you Work and the Endless list goes on. Don't take anything for Granted especially people. If someone isn't being nice to you. Forgive and Love them. Understand that they are struggling with something themselves in their own Lives. They don't mean to be nasty.

Towards you. It is because they are going through a traumatic time in their Life. In time they will get through this difficult time just like you will. Don't judge anyone. Accept people for how they are. We all have Unique Qualities to offer each other. Every person is Special Valuable Important Precious. Always Love your enemies. Look forward to the times you have with your Family and your Friends.

Make the most of every day of your Life. Organize good times with your Family and Friends. By doing interesting and exciting things with them. Do something kind for someone you know who is in need of help. Your Life is here for you to fulfill your Dreams. To have Wonderful Experiences that you will never ever Forget. Always Live your Days to the Fullest. God is in The Kingdom of Heaven. God will always be there for all of Eternity. God works through all of us as Human Beings. We have the choice to be kind to people or not.

When you can Forgive and Love people when they hurt you. Your Heart will be Filled with God's Everlasting Love Compassion Sympathy Empathy Kindness Goodness always and Forevermore. You will experience God's Loving Presence within yourself. God will Bless you and Reward you. With God's Loving Riches and Mercy. God loves those people who Believe in him. Who Live their Lives with Kindness Goodness Respect Grace Compassion Sympathy Empathy Forgiveness Acceptance Understanding. Towards their Fellow Man.

We are all important as Human Beings. We all have something to offer each other and to offer the World. There is always hope for everyone of us. Life is a Superb Gift from God. Your Life is here for you to Live it however you choose to. Think of other people's needs as well as your own. Other people are just as important as you are. Every person holds their own inner beauty goodness positivity. Usually when someone seems slightly abrupt. It is a reflection of how they are feeling within themselves. Learn not to take what people say to you personally. As we get older we learn not to take peoples negative words to heart. Like we did when we were younger.

We are Forever Learning how to improve and better ourselves. For better times to come in our Future. After you die your whole soul will be taken to The Kingdom of Heaven. Where Jesus will be seated at the right hand side of the Father God. Heaven will be brought to this Earth. Where you will Live with your Father God Almighty Forever and Ever and Ever. God is watching over you every day of your Life. God sees your intentions and motives towards how you treat other people. God knows how you feel within yourself. God is with you.

God absolutely loves you and adores you completely. God wants Good to happen to you. God will decide when it is time for you to join God in The Kingdom of Heaven. Believe in The Lord Jesus Christ Almighty and all will go well for you. Forgive and Love people who hurt you. Do something kind for them. Love your enemies. Continue to have days full of enjoyment satisfaction happiness. God is love.

That's what God wants for you. You have got all of the answers to what you are searching for in your Life. Have Understanding about where other people are coming from. With their point of views. This will help you in the long run in all kinds of beneficial ways. When you start to slightly feel affected by another persons comments towards you. Forgive and Love them by saying something nice to them. Even put a smile on your face. When you smile this says a lot about you.

It gives people the impression that you are a happy person who doesn't let anything bother you. Smiling is free and it makes you and other people happy. It also is a sign that you feel good within yourself. People love to see a smiling face. Don't worry anything in your Life. Be Happy and Content within yourself. Practice speaking positively about your Family and your Friends. What goes around comes around. Learn to use your sense of humour when you think it is appropriate. There is no need to take what people say to heart. If you think it might be slightly hurtful. People who are like this don't mean to hurt you. They are going through their own stuff in their own lives. All the experiences you have ever been through.

All of the things you have done in your Life has made you into the person you are to this day. You can choose to have a Positive Attitude with all that happens to you. When you are able to use your Positive Potentials with people and for yourself. You will see how much better you will feel about yourself. You will see how other people will respond towards you. They will do the same in return. When you are Positive Kind Loving Good Fair Just to everyone.

Then people will treat you in these Ways in return. What you give out you will always get back. As we get older we are gaining more skills of handling all kinds of people from different walks of Life. The more people you interact with at work. Where you study at your interests. Where you meet people socially. The more skills resources experiences you are dealing with these people. There is no need to Fear anything at all. Always be Fearless and Unafraid. God is there.

As long as you use your common sense with all that you do. Learn to accept things as they are if things don't turn out as you would of liked them to. Give it time and you will see how things will fall into Place Perfectly for you. You will be Pleasantly Surprised. You will have everything you could ever Possibly Ever Dream to have. In The Right and Best Time. Remember All Good Things Come to those Who Wait with Patience. You will have Blessings of Fulfillment Happiness.

Be Grateful Thankful Appreciative for every day you have. Enjoy every day of your Life. Fill your time up with things that you will get Pleasure and Satisfaction from. Live every day to the Fullest. This way you will feel good about what you have done. Learn to assert yourself when you feel like it is appropriate with people. Usually when someone says something hurtful to you. It is because they are a touch envious of what you have got in your Life. That they haven't got or it could be they are going through their own problems themselves. Having Understanding of other people where they are coming from. Will help you Enormously in the Long Run. Practice putting yourself in other peoples shoes. People like to be listened to.

And understood. We all want to feel liked accepted wanted loved nurtured understood validated cherished treasured by other people. God sees everything you do. When you have faith love hope in God. It will make you a loving forgiving accepting understanding positive kind hearted good willed fair just person. God loves you so much. God has got a lot of exciting meaningful rewarding times ahead for you to come in your Future. Work on helping and improving yourself.

In the situations you are in and when you are alone. Put your best efforts into everything that you do. None of us really know how long we have got to live on this Earth. This should encourage you to have Great Fabulous Joyful Peaceful Happy Go Lucky Times Every Day. Do all that you have ever Dreamed of. Make all of your Dreams come true.

Review Requested:

We'd like to know if you enjoyed the book.
Please consider leaving a review on the platform from which you purchased the book.

CPSIA information can be obtained
at www.ICGtesting.com
Printed in the USA
LVHW032230250521
688475LV00005B/197

9 781682 354728